NO REGRETS
Eleven Steps To Live Your Best Life

Eddie Tomberlin

COWCATCHER Publications

BLUFFTON, SC

Copyright © 2014 by **Eddie Tomberlin**

All rights reserved. No part of this publication may be reproduced, distributed or transmitted in any form or by any means, without prior written permission.

Eddie Tomberlin/COWCATCHER Publications
11 Concession Oak Drive
Bluffton, SC/29909
www.do-the-write-thing.com

Publisher's Note: This is a work created by Eddie Tomberlin. All scripture quotations are from the Holy Bible, New International Version, Zondervan Bible Publishers, Grand Rapids, Michigan, USA. Copyright © 1973, 1978, 1984 by International Bible Society.

Book Layout © 2014 BookDesignTemplates.com

NO REGRETS/ Eddie Tomberlin. -- 1st ed.
ISBN 978-0-9960533-0-3

ACKNOWLEDGEMENTS

I'd like to acknowledge and thank a few people who helped make this book a reality. I'd like to extend special thanks to my friends Craig and Cheryl Rymal for their early review of this work and ongoing support and encouragement. Also, I have to thank Jodie Randisi for her editing and organization of the overall manuscript. Where the book flows and makes sense, it is to her credit. Where it does not, I take all the blame.

I'd like to acknowledge some people who, in many different ways, have helped shape me as a person and a minister. Thank you to my all-time favorite teacher, Elaine Stephens, for ever since my high school days, reading early manuscripts and being encouraging even though we both know you wanted to pull out the red pen and make me start all over. To My Grace Culture, you are my daily inspiration and a joy to serve alongside. To Elders Ted White and Ryan Burke, you provided much-needed reassurance as you stayed and believed all these years in spite of naysayers. To Victor Polero, Montel Powers, Matt Rahn and Dell Sheffield, I must thank you for watching over the flock as shepherds with such care and compassion.

To my father and mother-in-law, Charles and Linda Green, thank you for trusting me with your daughter and grandchildren, and also for giving me my first shot at fulltime ministry. To our friends Clint Proudfoot and Tammie Hall—your constant care and protection of LaDonna and me throughout the years has given us such value, we can never repay it. Thank you Susannah Jarvis for praying over my family and me and for being our spiritual advisor, psychiatrist and personal physician. To my parents, Bill and Joyce Tomberlin—thank you for continually praying for me and supporting me in spite of mistakes and detours along the way. To my brothers Mickey, Gary and Robbie—thank you for teaching me what ministry is all about. To my children Mandy and Jareb—you make me so proud that I get to be your dad. To my son-in-law Matt and daughter-in-law Amanda—on behalf of LaDonna, our children and myself, we could not have asked for better people to share life with. To my pride and joy and first grandbaby Kaiden—Pop Pop will continue to spoil you no matter what the peanut gallery says. And to my precious wife LaDonna—it would take a lifetime to share what you mean to me. Your love, patience and support are undying, and I'm still surprised you chose me.

There are others I could and should name but I'll leave room for them in my next book. I love you all and am honored to have you in my life.

—EDDIE

CONTENTS

INTRODUCTION 5
CHALLENGE THE STATUS QUO 9
LEARN TO EXPLORE 17
DREAM AGAIN 29
GO WHERE THE ACTION IS 39
LEARN TO FORGIVE 49
EMBRACE YOUR PAST 59
LEARN TO ELIMINATE 67
MIND YOUR BUSINESS 75
LEARN TO LAUGH 81
LEARN TO DISCERN 91
GOD'S WILL REVEALED 97
DISCUSSION QUESTIONS 103

FOREWORD

I believe there are persons in the throes of life decisions who are challenged in how they will respond to a life-altering bit of information. For example, I once heard a minister describing the response of Peter and John to the news that Jesus' tomb was empty in The Gospel of John, chapter twenty. John outran Peter, but only stood at the entrance looking in. Peter came soon after, but unlike John, he went all the way in and saw what John didn't see. John eventually went in and saw what Peter saw. I am convinced that an unspoken desire, when verbalized, will trigger a set of events in our lives that alters an entire landscape.

Four desperate men came to a sobering conclusion one day. They were faced with the possibility of imminent death from one of two choices. The first choice required doing nothing but remaining in the status quo. The second choice involved risk, and the almost certainty of immediate death, but this is the one they chose. The outcome of this choice produced an amazing windfall of wealth for the four adventurers and a miraculous deliverance for an entire city already on life support. But that's another story for another time.

I believe there is a destiny waiting for those who will choose a particular path, simply because the alternative is too difficult to accept. For those four starving men, the remote possibility of a better life outweighed the certainty of approaching death. And like the four men who said something, our words can create worlds—worlds we could have never known existed if we hadn't said something. I am absolutely convinced that nothing happens in the kingdom until something is declared or spoken. The hidden power in *saying something* triggers events in the universe that conspire with God's purpose to bring you to the edge, where you can see a world you always knew existed. Living with no regrets is not a life of foolish dissipation, but rather a life of joyous adventure.

However, if you want to explore new territory, it's best to have an experienced guide who can show you how to see the new world in front of you. In the book of The Acts of the Apostles, there is an account of Philip, the evangelist, hearing an Ethiopian dignitary reading from the Book of Isaiah. He asked him if he understood what he was reading. The official replied, "How can I understand unless someone explains it to me?" The word *explain* in the original Greek means to *lead the way*. Receiving assistance from an experienced guide is always beneficial.

Through the years, it has been my privilege and honor to give pastoral care to a number of significant leaders in the body of Christ, both nationally and internationally. Bishop Eddie Tomberlin is one of those leaders. I respect his honesty and integrity, which is contained in an amazing mix of creativity and excellence. And yet he remains tremendously humble. In the following pages, you will find in Bishop Eddie Tomberlin an experienced guide, who will see you safely and sanely through what some would call dangerous territory. He has lived it, loved it and proven the worth of it. It is my hope that his words will produce a new company of individuals who will dare to challenge the status quo and live a dynamic life with no regrets.

Bishop Joseph L. Garlington, Sr.
Presiding Bishop
Covenant Church of Pittsburgh
Reconciliation! Ministries International

When smiling Eddie Tomberlin strolled into my high school English class I knew him by word of mouth only, and I leave it to his readers to determine what those descriptions might have been. As the year progressed, I came to love and respect this young man; even then, the obvious call of God was upon him. Memories have stood the test of time, and I have been blessed by this relationship. We have shared struggles and triumphs as God continues to use him mightily. Reading this book, I realize even more so, God speaks through Eddie Tomberlin, and most importantly, He is speaking to me.

—Elaine Stephens

English professor, South Georgia State College

INTRODUCTION

I've always been a risk-taker. I love to explore new things. To some people my attraction to adventure might give the impression that I have a touch of Attention Deficit Disorder (ADD). If I were forced to label myself, a more accurate description of my God-given nature might be DAA, Devoted Adventurer Attitude. I approach everything with the attitude that when I'm done with whatever it is I'm doing, I can, and will, walk away with no regrets.

I've made the decision to live a life with no regrets. It's not about arrogance. It's about challenging the status quo with boldness. I guess you could call me a "leave it all on the field" kind of guy. Leaving it all on the field means you don't end feeling as if you could have given more. You don't leave knowing you played it safe when you had the opportunity for something greater. If you've given everything you have to give, then there will be no room for questions about what you could have or might have done.

This book addresses exactly how to both acquire and expand an attitude of no regrets. Simply put, *No Regrets* outlines eleven principles proven to remove obstacles to success in life. I've included practical steps designed to strengthen us spiritually, emotionally and physically. Each chapter was written to prepare readers for future adventures. To illustrate these eleven important concepts, I've included stories and life experiences that will help readers understand and appreciate what it means to live life with no regrets. In the end, I want people to joyfully take advantage of all future adventurous opportunities.

Perhaps this is a good time to address how I think readers can get the most from this book. You might consider *not* reading this book cover to cover, although that is certainly one way to approach a good book. Instead, may I suggest finding a chapter with a title that piques your interest and start there? In other words, as the author, I trust your level of interest to guide you through the book. I also recommend that readers highlight passages that are especially meaningful. Whatever you do, don't leave anything on the field. Go for it!

May I also suggest that you don't read this book with just yourself in mind? Think of others who would appreciate some knowledgeable encouragement. If you've been looking for a book to stimulate small group discussion, then you've found it. Look no further. Check out the WORDS OF WISDOM and DISCUSSION QUESTIONS at the end of each chapter. I'm sure you'll agree that when we share life experiences in small group discussion, everyone benefits.

Also, you'll see that this book was written from my perspective as a believer and follower of Jesus Christ. Hold on. You might want to hit the pause button if that turns you off. I did not write this book to win converts or make disciples. I'm simply putting my words out there to inspire new thoughts in those who are willing to investigate new beliefs. I reference scripture because I use the Bible for personal development and wisdom. If you have no religious affiliation, or if you don't believe in God, I'm confident you'll find the wisdom found in these eleven principles both relevant and practical.

And by the way, please feel free to recycle my words in any way you see fit, including tweets and so on. Sharing something you read and liked, now that's something I highly encourage.

I'm grateful you've taken the time to read this introduction. I hope and pray you'll finish the book and let me know how you were able to take meaningful steps toward living a life with **NO REGRETS**. I look forward to hearing how you were able to, by God's grace, become more of the person you were created to be.

CHAPTER ONE

CHALLENGE THE STATUS QUO

Here's to the crazy ones. The misfits. The rebels. The troublemakers. The round pegs in the square holes. The ones who see things differently. They're not fond of rules. And they have no respect for the status quo. You can quote them, disagree with them, glorify or vilify them. About the only thing you can't do is ignore them. Because they change things. They push the human race forward. And while some may see them as the crazy ones, we see genius. Because the people who are crazy enough to think they can change the world, are the ones who do.

—Apple Inc.

Leave It All on the Field

I grew up in a neighborhood populated by an unusual cast of characters. Together with my brothers, there were enough of us to field an entire football team, offense and defense.

Let's see, there were the Collins brothers, Kelly, Keith and Kent. Kelly was an insanely good athlete. Keith would chew on his index finger when he got mad. Kent, well, he liked Mary Jane—the herb, not the girl. We also had the Hall brothers, Mickey and Michael, both mean as a snake, extremely intense and good enough to have on your team. They weren't afraid to fight anyone. Then there was Nathan, the neighborhood nerd, or so we thought until he put a fanny whooping on Michael that none of us would ever soon forget.

Also in our posse, we had the Williams/Smith stepbrothers, Smokey, Hank, Charlie and Cindy. I have to include Cindy as one of the boys because she could pretty much whoop us all. Smokey was an incredible baseball player, Hank knew all the cuss words, and Charlie had a serious speech impediment. When Charlie cussed with a lisp (or whatever it was he had), it was downright funny.

We also had two used car salesmen, Jay and Jimmy. That's what we called them anyway. They operated a little thrift store in their house, and for some reason, a whole bunch of kids would buy their junk at retail prices. Then we had Leslie, Jeff, Edward, Mike and another Eddie. Rickey and Robbie's dad owned a gas station where we sometimes got free Fudgsicles. Troy, Tony and Chris and the rest of us played every kind of ball game or sport you could think of, and we played all the time.

With this crew of reckless criminals, one thing was certain. Whether we won or lost to a group of kids from another part of town, the field would become a war zone. These crazy guys were built for intensity, insanity and injury. Taking big risks was a part of their daily routine. Every one of us wanted to win.

As we grew older, most of us switched from neighborhood ball to high school sports. Some went on to play for collegiate and professional sports teams. Needless to say, these guys didn't give up their tenacity and commitment to leave it all on the field. In fact, they were even more single-minded as they gained more experience. For us, playing sports with a no regrets attitude was instinctive. No one taught us to give blood, sweat and tears; we just did.

Looking back, I realize I was part of a strange, eclectic group of kids. We came from assorted backgrounds, yet we played, fought, cried and laughed all together with no regrets. Our young lives were consumed with playing. I remember the mass quantities of B&F hamburgers we devoured, the hazardous ramps we jumped, the bones we broke, and the hundreds of baseball, basketball, and football games we played with steadfast intensity.

Perhaps we were afforded this time because we did not have video games or smart phones. We enjoyed life as it came to us. It didn't matter if someone's parents had or didn't have money. It didn't matter where we slept at night, or what food we ate. It certainly didn't make any difference if a kid wore name brand clothing or last year's hand-me-downs. We were a band of brothers who always left everything on the field, one hundred percent. We didn't challenge ourselves to become adventurous. Nor did we need extra motivation to become adventurers. We just were.

I'm convinced many people have forgotten how it feels to be adventurous and creative. When that happens, I believe we become the opposite of how God intends for us to be. We are created in His image, and He is, after all, the God of creation.

Make the Decision

To leave it all on the field means you've made a decision to give every ounce of effort and energy to win or complete a particular task. Knowing you've given your all to fulfill a dream, or to accomplish a risky feat also means you've effectively challenged the status quo. You've been provoked to move beyond the norm.

I've been provoked to move beyond the norm many times, but as an example, I'd like to share with you how the Holy Spirit helped me make the decision to leave a church where I was the lead pastor of a great congregation. In a very short period of time, our church became one of the state's largest and fastest growing churches in our denomination. We had become serious players in our community. We were moving fast, in what some might consider a supernatural growth spurt.

Call it a prompting, or unction, or whatever, all I know is, it was happening to me. My wife Ladonna was also being provoked. We knew the time had come to withdraw our affiliation with the denomination, which meant leaving the church we were leading. After making the announcement, we faced expected as well as unexpected challenges. There were uncomfortable transitions, trials of our faith, rumors that led to heartache and betrayals, and way too many sleepless nights.

God had given Ladonna and me a new directive. We made the decision to obey the Holy Spirit as He guided us to a new path. As expected, we continue to see God's plan unfold. I am now with some of the finest people on the planet, to which I affectionately refer to as my Grace Culture, also the name of our non-denominational church.

Why would I use this as an example to introduce readers to the concept of challenging the status quo while leaving it all on the field? I share this because my entire life has been wrapped up in ministry. My primary connection to ministry for 46 years came through our denomination. It was all I had ever known. I was somewhat sheltered. I could not see the greater challenges and opportunities waiting for me outside the norm. When asked by church officials, "What do you think you can do outside the denomination that you can't do in it?" I replied, "I don't know. I've never tried."

I understand that what I had been connected to for so many years was just a tributary in a huge river. My comfort zone needed to be confronted. And for a period of time, while we found our way into new territory, things were unfamiliar and uncomfortable. But it was the right thing to do.

Here are some questions for you to consider:

What haven't you done?

What does your comfort zone look like?

What have you been doing for the last year, five years, ten years that has kept you comfortable, or should I say non-adventurous?

A Greater Power

There's a greater power working in me that won't allow me to live comfortably in the status quo. It is through Christ Jesus and His grace that I'm given strength to do what I couldn't do on my own. It sounds pretty simple because it is simple.

Who is Christ? Let me explain. Christ is not Jesus' last name. The word Christ comes from the Greek word **Khristos**. It is the noun use of an adjective meaning *'anointed,'* from **khriein** *'anoint,'* which when translated into Hebrew is **māšīaḥ** *'Messiah.'* When we receive Christ into our lives, when we come into the salvation knowledge of Jesus, we receive more than forgiveness for our sins. It's about having unmerited favor with God. We gain His Christ, His anointing,

His authority, His ability and potential, His imagination...all given to us by the Spirit now dwelling in us.

Romans 8:11 tells us, *And if the Spirit of him who raised Jesus from the dead is living in you, he who raised Christ from the dead will also give life to your mortal bodies through his Spirit who lives in you.*

Let me explain how this verse applies to our lives as Christians. The same Spirit that raised Jesus from the dead lives in us. We received Jesus into our lives and His Christ (anointing) comes with Him and resides in us. We are able to accomplish (and be) everything He desires.

Christ in us provokes us to live beyond the norm and past the status quo. Ephesians 3:20-21 tells us, *Now to him who is able to do immeasurably more than all we ask or imagine, according to his power that is at work within us, to him be glory in the church and in Christ Jesus throughout all generations, for ever and ever! Amen.*

I take that to mean God is greater than my imagination. In other words, He's better than me at imagining things I could do. Now that's pretty exciting. Because of God's anointing, we're truly able to do all things through Christ who strengthens us.

Has anyone ever challenged you to live beyond the status quo? If not, may I be the first? If you feel as though you're living with mediocrity, confined by a mundane existence, then it's time for you to dream again. It's time to consider how you can live outside your comfort zone. It's time to revisit what it feels like to be adventurous. If your dreams are hiding behind the status quo, then it's time to leave it all on the field and head for uncharted waters.

I'll close with some good advice. I recommend you take steps in a new direction away from the status quo.

WORDS OF WISDOM

It's never too late to start living a life with *NO REGRETS!*

DISCUSSION QUESTIONS

1.1 Have you ever "left it all on the field" before? If so, describe the circumstances and your reasons.

1.2 What, if anything, are you holding back from God? What are you holding back from others, especially those with obvious needs?

1.3 What would it look like if you left it all on the field for your church or your family? What would change?

1.4 Recall a time when you challenged the status quo. How did you feel before, during and after? What might not have happened if you had played it safe?

CHAPTER TWO

LEARN TO EXPLORE

A season of suffering is a small assignment when compared to the reward. Rather than begrudge your problem, explore it. Ponder it. And most of all, use it. Use it to the glory of God.

—Max Lucado.

Safe, Secure and Miserable
Someone told me that if I just kept my nose clean, played by the rules and continued to help others accomplish their agenda, I would eventually have a chance at a real promotion. The promotion, I was told, came with political perks and all kinds of advantages. All I had to do was keep it between the lines and not cause any waves. If I did that I would enjoy even more security, friends, and opportunities than I already had.

Mind you, for nearly a half century, I enjoyed being raised in a denominational church and later taking a leadership position in that same denomination. For twenty-six years, I was an ordained Bishop serving in full-time ministry. With my connections and work ethic, I was confident certain relationships would lead to a bigger church in a bigger town with more potential. If things didn't work out, my organization would take care of placing me where I would be best suited. I had a respectable safety net.

However, not making waves and just getting by has always been hard for me. I've always felt comfortable on the frontline, pushing the envelope, if you will. I love to search things out for myself. I'm not one to take someone's word on a subject. If it doesn't feel right or sit well, I want to find out why it doesn't feel right. I ask a lot of questions. And when I explore new thoughts, deeper truths, or radical shifts, I expect to uncover answers that do feel right and sit well.

Before I go any further, let me make something crystal clear. I do not want to be misunderstood. I believe denominations and organizational fellowships are good, just not good for me. Even though I was highly successful in every position I held, after a while, staying connected to a denomination didn't feel right. It wasn't because I believed I was affiliated with a bad organization. My sense of ownership didn't line up with my personal philosophy or revelation. I felt compelled to explore a new direction and longed for a release within my assignment.

I firmly believe our approach to life, including relationships, work situations, education, and so on, should be explored for ourselves. For example, if someone has something to say about another person, either positive or negative, I still like to form my own opinion. I refuse to cast judgment, create an opinion, or blame someone through the filter of another person's experience. It's unhealthy and dangerous. Their offense can become your offense. I'm thankful we all have opinions, but we also all have noses, and yours doesn't work for me.

It's free advice. Take it or leave it, but I highly recommend you take it!

Traditions of Men

I was taught that even though we're saved by grace through faith, we still had to work hard to please God. It was imperative to do all the right things, wear the right clothes, and stay away from the wrong people and places. I was told, and I'm using proper southern Georgia vernacular here, "Don't hang out with them sinners."

Getting into heaven was all about being sanctified, not doing certain things while doing the right things. We were assured that if we prayed every night before we went to sleep and asked God to forgive us of the sins we had committed earlier, there might be a chance to make it through the pearly gates of heaven.

From a very young age, I was exposed to a long list of traditions outlined by the spiritual leaders and men of God in my life. I remember one evangelist who came to my home church every year. He seemed determined to make us so afraid of God that we'd end up living in church and praying all the time, wearing sackcloth and sitting in a pile of ashes. Participating in worldly entertainment, in his view, would send us straight to hell. In his view, worldly entertainment included going to high school football games. Unfortunately for those of us players and fans of the game, the stadium was located right across the street from our church.

Brother WhatzHizName would routinely preach fiery, hell and damnation sermons. On more than one occasion, I remember him finding a way to insert a discourse about how women should (and should not) wear their hair. He preached some harsh stuff. "Make-up, doncha ya know, is devil's paint!" he would declare.

I'd just like to say, the Lord knows some of those women could have benefited from a bit of that paint, and I know for a fact I wasn't the only kid thinking that. If you were caught inside a movie house, you could be excommunicated from the church. I was eternally grateful we had a drive-in outdoor movie theater in our county. Again, not the only kid.

The evangelist would preach from the book of Revelation just to ignite any remaining or repressed fear in the congregation. I remember watching people run down to the altars like they were already on fire. He'd shout, "What if Jesus came back tonight? Would He see you in all your sin? Will you be left here to go through the tribulation?" We knew our ultimate demise was to burn in hell where there would be weeping and gnashing of teeth. *Oh my, not I!* As children, we were literally afraid of God. We thought God was out to get us.

After many years of believing God was mad at me, I decided to examine these traditions of men. Apparently, some evangelical rule makers didn't know that the traditions of man invalidate the word of God. In the seventh chapter of Mark's gospel in verse 13 we are told, *Thus you nullify the word of God by your tradition that you have handed down.*

I decided to do a little exploring on my own. Something about a loving God being disappointed in me all the time and wanting to send me to hell just didn't make sense. It didn't sound right. It didn't feel right.

My interest concerning the depth of the grace of God was ignited when I began listening to the teachings of a woman of great faith whose name I won't mention. Sitting under a woman's Bible teaching was (and still is in some small circles) not acceptable in that denomination. Men hold the platform leadership positions in the church, and women preachers are not recognized. Women, I was told, are not viewed as equals in spiritual matters because men alone had the authority to teach the word of God. Nevertheless, this woman's teaching caused faith to rise up in my inner man. Her message sat right with me.

Eventually, as a result of the revelation I was receiving, I knew the time would come when I would be pressed to make a life-altering decision. This fresh, progressive exposure to God's radical grace challenged my belief system. I had to choose between staying connected in the safety of my status quo, or go forward with nothing but God. As I'm sure you've already figured out, I chose just GOD, nothing else. It was time for me to leave the traditions of men behind.

Moments of Clarity

Immediately after making the decision to give up man's traditions and follow just God, I had only one question…what now? Even though I could never rightfully compare myself with our forefather Abraham (Abram), I do have an inkling of how he must have felt when God told him to leave his homeland.

Genesis 12:1-2 tells us, *The LORD had said to Abram, 'Leave your country, your people and your father's household and go to the land I will show you. I will make you into a great nation and I will bless you; I will make your name great, and you will be a blessing.'*

Essentially, when God told Abram to leave his friends, family and possessions and move to an unknown destination,

He was telling Abram to leave the status quo for a life with no regrets.

As it turns out, when I was considering removing myself from our denomination, I had some serious thoughts (or reservations) about how this scripture applied to my situation and me. *Hold on! Things are good right here, God. My family is doing well and our future looks pretty secure.*

But that was not Abram's response. Abraham's destiny was bound to his obedience and God's favor worked in tandem with Abraham's mobility. When God changed his name from Abram to Abraham, the meaning of his name changed to reflect his new identity, father of many nations. Abraham became mobile, did everything God instructed him to do, and as a result, found himself in the hands of God's favor.

Abraham met his decision with clarity and a certain amount of ease. As far as I can tell, he was not at all surprised by God's command to leave home. I never thought about it this way until one evening when I was reading through the book of Genesis. A new thought struck me. *Wouldn't there be some level of excitement, or fear, or panic, or all of the above, when someone receives marching orders from God?*

It appears Abram already had a fairly well established relationship with God. He asked no questions. He didn't look around to find where the voice was coming from. He didn't run away in fear. He didn't hide from God. What he did was offer an immediate response.

The LORD had said to Abram, 'Leave your country, your people and your father's household and go to the land I will show you. I will make you into a great nation and I will bless you; I will make your name great, and you will be a blessing.

I will bless those who bless you, and whoever curses you I will curse; and all people on the earth will be blessed through you.' Genesis 12: 1-3

So Abram left, as the LORD had told him... verse 4.

I believe Abram's speedy response was a reflection of his intimate relationship with God. I'm going to make the assumption that these two had been talking for quite some time prior to this conversation. Abram's response spoke volumes. It said, "I know you. I trust you. I will follow you."

Like Abraham, a willingness to follow God has transported me into unknown territory, and I can say with clarity, I've had no regrets.

Audacious Prayers

Another moment of clarity came to me after hearing a young preacher speak on the subject of audacious prayers. Audacious prayers are bold, confident, courageous and unafraid. That level of prayer, or should I say communication and communion with God, comes from a genuine relationship. In his sermon, the preacher stated that praying audacious prayers would result in the following:

1. You will have the confidence to know that nothing is impossible with God.
2. You will gain the necessary clarity to see the next step God is calling you to take.
3. You will find the courage to do anything He tells you to do.

After praying daily for clear direction along with the wisdom to obey God's leading and the courage to be moveable, I did hear God say, *Now you move. It's time to establish and ignite a grace culture that is the true expression of the Church I am building.*

I have to say, God never told me to build a church. He takes care of that according to scripture. In Matthew 16:18, Jesus tells Peter, *I will build my church and the gates of Hades will not overcome it.* God's word to me was to establish and ignite a culture that would be **an expression of His church.**

And there you have it. Our moments of clarity had come full circle. We had to move out of our comfortable "home" and move on. Courage showed up and produced new confidence and our journey with Grace Culture had begun.

I'm convinced that life's greatest challenges are found in the initial step that change requires. The future God has for you requires a personalized step of faith. And by the way, every passageway to a life with no regrets will be paved with faith. The dilemma most people face is being human, meaning it's hard to have and maintain faith just to get by in this life and not go crazy in the process. It's even more difficult to have faith to live a life without regrets. However, great opportunities will present themselves when you face God and ask Him, "Now what?" In doing so, you've made the decision to take the step where there's nowhere else to turn but to God. The good news is God rewards that kind of faith.

Verse 6 of Hebrews 11 tells us, *And without faith it is impossible to please God, because anyone who comes to him must believe that he exists and that he rewards those who earnestly seek him.*

Let me interject a word of caution here. When you trust God and obey His Word, don't be surprised when, as you're walking out your destiny, you start to feel as if you're in the middle of a lake rowing a boat tossed by waves produced by a great storm. That will happen. It's a given. God will ask you to step out of your boat like He did Peter. "Come," He will bid you.

However, when our steps are ordered by the Lord, walking on water in the middle of a hurricane will be like taking a leisurely stroll in the park. The more you get to know Him, the more your faith grows. The more your faith grows, the easier it is to step out of your boat and walk on water.

God Is

Let me simplify things for a moment. Living a life without regrets is not about believing God will do something for you, or that you can accomplish anything in or by yourself. It is about believing that God *is* God. It's truly that simple.

Jesus didn't come only to forgive mankind's collective sins, or transgressions. He also came to deal with our sin of unbelief as individuals. To believe Him translates to our salvation. The issue is not how much faith you have, but rather where, or in whom, your faith is placed. God doesn't work in proportion to your need of Him but in proportion to your knowledge of Him. The more you get to know Him, the more your faith grows.

It may be that you need to come to grips with the truth that you can't dream big dreams. When compared to the potential God has placed within us, our dreams do tend to be rather small. Still, a life of no regrets begins when you decide to trust God's dream for you, which will be beyond what you imagine will be good, or even perfect for your future. The question is how do we tap into God's potential and realize His dream for us?

Living a life with no regrets begins with exploring. Try exploring your future after removing negative thoughts of what could have been, might have been, or should have been. Acknowledge that your life's story has many unfulfilled chapters. God has written several, perhaps many, adventurous chapters you have not yet experienced. God loves you and has an abundant life planned for you. The key is to get to know Him, grow in faith and take a step out of the boat away from the status quo. Then watch how life unfolds, opportunities present themselves and adventures begin to accumulate.

WORDS OF WISDOM

Change happens, so don't fight it. Accept change as a great tool. Change helps you give up what you are for what you will become.

DISCUSSION QUESTIONS

2.1. Have you ever felt safe, secure and miserable? If so, what were the circumstances?

2.2. Describe your religious upbringing. If you were not raised in a denominational church or religious family, did you ever have the inclination to explore religious studies?

2.3. If you were raised in a denominational church, did you ever question any of the church's teachings or values?

2.4. Describe a time when you prayed for direction and followed God's leading.

2.5. Have you ever made a substantial change in your life that resulted in people disagreeing with your actions? If so, were the results encouraging or disheartening?

2.6. When was the last time you explored something new? Describe what you did and how you benefited.

CHAPTER THREE

DREAM AGAIN

A The Queen of Hearts said, "Sometimes I've believed as many as six impossible things before breakfast."
—Lewis Carroll

Boy with Six Toes

Remember Mickey? I mentioned him earlier. He was one of the hearty neighborhood characters from my childhood. Mickey stood out in our small town of Baxley, Georgia not because he was the best looking or the coolest kid around. In reality, he was a kid with extremely limited resources living in a dysfunctional home. He had the poor physical hygiene to prove it, too. Still, he made an impression.

Let's see, how can I explain this. The kid had the mouth of a sailor on him, was mean as a snake, had six toes on one foot, and walked around barefoot every day from March until sometime in October when the weather turned too cold to go shoeless in south Georgia. I was always a little afraid of him but for some unexplainable reason, I had a strange admiration for him. His home life was a mess--an older brother who beat him up almost daily, six toes on one foot—yet he had this uncommon ability to act out his dreams.

Mickey refused to lose and fought with anyone who tried to deny him victories. When we played football, Mickey turned into star quarterback Roger Staubach. When we played baseball, he transformed into first baseman Don Mattingly. In basketball, he became NBA star player Larry Byrd. When we played Army, Mickey was Sergeant Sam Troy from RAT Patrol. When we played cowboys and Indians, he was the Lone Ranger. In our day, these guys were the best players and coolest characters on television.

Mickey filtered life through his own lens of creativity. For example, his bicycle was a creation of different parts he put together from whatever he found lying around in a junk pile. To him, and to us, his bike was a masterpiece. Naturally, it was built for handling top speeds and extreme ramps made for soaring through the air.

No task was too hard for Mickey. He was determined to make the most of his young life. No adventure too big, no dirt pile too messy. Mickey wanted all the kids to join him in his world of play and make believe. Every time he knocked on our door, my brothers and I knew we were about to experience another adventure, one that could only be conjured up in the mind of six-toed Mickey who jokingly acknowledged his unique physical attribute often. This was only one of the reasons we admired him so much. Our quaint little corner of town wouldn't have been the same without Mickey.

What would it be like to make believe again, play again, dream again, and take as few baths as possible? What would that be like? Some people say young life should include adventures featuring dirt and mishaps due to radical risk-taking, and ours did. To us, Mickey symbolized adventure. He showed us what it meant to be a dreamer. Despite his dysfunctional underprivileged life, the kid with six toes knew what it meant to dream.

How do you tell a kid with that kind of tenacity and determination that he can't or shouldn't dream big dreams? The answer is simple. You don't because you can't. Determination breeds confidence and when a child acquires even a little confidence, he digs in even more. And once a child has decided to plant himself into a situation, tenacity takes root, after which you would have a terrible time trying to convince them they might fail. Failure is not an option. Quitting is not an option. Clever kids might lose a few skirmishes but they'll never lose the war, so to speak.

Do you remember learning how to ride a bike? As kids, nearly all of us were filled with determination to master the skill of riding a bike without training wheels. We got back up on our bikes with two scraped knees and wounded pride because we saw other kids riding their bikes. No way were we going to sit around while friends and neighbors rode their way to freedom. We told ourselves, "I can do this! I will do this!"

People are affected when they watch great athletes, read fantastic stories, and listen to inspirational speeches. They imagine themselves in the situation and think, "I could do that." Dreaming big prepares our minds for the adventures that lie ahead, and that's a good thing.

One more thing you ought to consider. Life gets interesting when the dream becomes our vision. It's when the dream moves eighteen inches down from our heads into our hearts— then it becomes our vision. Vision has a tendency to create motivation. Once imagination transforms into motivation, momentum develops. And once momentum has reached its boiling point, an explosion of creativity forces its way to the surface. You'll find yourself standing at the crossroads of change and new possibilities.

Dream Anyway

For some reason, as people grow older people they tend to stop dreaming. Maybe you've been exposed to naysayers and dream killers. Perhaps someone told you that you shouldn't dream or that your dream couldn't be accomplished. Perhaps they were effective when they pointed out your disadvantages, challenges and lack of potential. But I say DREAM ANYWAY!

Don't cower under small-minded thinkers and loud-mouthed pessimists. Dream on! Dreams are meant to inspire us to see and accomplish greater things. Every inspiration we have should be met with desire…desire to do more, be more, give more, love more, serve more, and make more. I'm saying dream beyond the here and now. Envision yourself in a better place spiritually, physically, emotionally and financially. Dream big. Think outside the box and let imagination collide with creativity. Becoming the person you were designed to be works this way, and it starts with dreaming.

The word IMPOSSIBLE should inspire us. Stay determined when others tell you, "No way. That's not possible." If someone says you can't, or it's too late, or I wouldn't if I were you, tell them, "Sorry, you're too late." Why? Because dreams are the images God gives to steer you to the finished project. In other words, in the spirit, you've been there done that.

Let me explain it this way. Our physical and emotional being has to catch up with our eternal spirit being. Our creator God lives in the eternal now, which is where our spirits live. We can access the eternal now and experience a connection with God when we learn to tap into our divinely created spirit. Every time we dream, we could be looking into a future that already exists in the spiritual realm.

Have you ever experienced a déjà vu moment when you look around and say to yourself, wait a minute, this feels really familiar? You've probably told someone, "I've been here before," or, "I've experienced this before." This is a result of your deep subconscious mind having been *there* before you arrived *there* physically. What exists in the spiritual realm isn't bound by time restraints. Human beings, however, are limited to time and space.

Remember, God lives in the eternal now and when we dream we could be looking at future experiences. Dreams have the potential to set us up for incredible manifestations of amazing accomplishments, so don't let anyone talk you out of your good future, which has already been established.

Jeremiah 29, verse 11 tells us, *"For I know the plans I have for you," declares the LORD, "plans to prosper you and not to harm you, plans to give you hope and a future."* And then later, in Jeremiah 33, verses 2 and 3, the Bible tells us, *This is what the LORD says, he who made the earth, the LORD who formed it and established it–the LORD is his name: "Call to me and I will answer you and tell you great and unsearchable things you do not know."*

All that to say, allow your imagination to meet with your dreams. Permit yourself to see your future unfold right before your subconscious eyes. This is how we give birth to something here in our physical world that already exists in the spiritual world. Dream on!

Bucket List

Like Mickey, we ought to see each day through the lens of unbridled, spontaneous adventure. If we did that, every undertaking would become a quest for the lost treasure leading to a supernaturally joy-filled life. Of course, how you approach life will determine your outcome. If you're not sure how you approach life, it might be time to formulate a bucket list. A bucket list will reveal what drives you.

A bucket list is simply the things you'd like to do before you die. If you've seen or heard about the movie *The Bucket List* starring Morgan Freeman and Jack Nicholson, you know how these two characters were driven by the thought of their impending deaths. As they approached what they thought was the end of their lives, they were forced to consider how to best spend their time.

What about you? If you knew death was right around the corner, who would you call, what would you do, where would you go, and who would you spend time with? For most of us, this is not our last couple of days or weeks on earth, yet living a life with no regrets can't start soon enough. I, for one, don't want to be driven by the thought of my last days, final hours or an incurable disease.

And by the way, it's okay to modify what drives you. What motivated you in the past, may be different from what motivates you now. As you grow and change, you'll find interests and passions will evolve. For example, my ambitions shifted in a great way the moment I held my grandchild for the first time. I vividly remember tears falling from my face onto his little pink cheek. In that moment, it was as if the Lord said to me, "Just as your impassioned tear dropped onto the sweet face of that precious little baby, may your same passion for life drop into the hearts of the generations who will come after you."

In that moment, I became even more mindful of what I would leave behind for our children and our children's children. How could I live within the status quo with no real passion for life? I could not tolerate my successors becoming the byproducts of my regret, fear and missed opportunities. Our children deserve better. It was my job to convey what living with no regrets looked and felt like.

Here's a question for you—when you see opportunities, do you view them as just another thing you have to do? Or, when opportunities present themselves, do you view them as something you *get* to do? If you're living a life with no regrets, then nothing you do can be viewed as routine. It's quite the opposite. Changing your perspective from "I have to" to "I get to" means no obstacle or challenge is unwanted. With this attitude, you get to go to school or your job. Make the shift and you'll find life becomes a whole lot more interesting.

Spirit, Soul and Body

Making the choice to live a full life is not about reading then adopting the latest self-help program or diet. Living without regret means making thoughtful decisions to be the person God intends you to be on a daily basis. Exercise and self-help programs, diets and books will help keep you physically fit and healthy, but your decision to become a participant in God's plan for your life speaks to your inner man.

I believe we were born for adventure and designed for association. Your soul (your mind, will and emotions) wants to fill an empty space that was inherently created just by being born. The solution is to connect your spirit with God's. When you do this, you can experience God's innovative plan for your life.

I like to say it this way—you are a spirit, you possess a soul, and you live in a body. We are three-part beings. When you become born again through Christ, your spirit is saved, but your soul is being saved as you renew your mind and eventually, your body will be saved at the resurrection, or when you get to heaven. It's important to realize that life gets difficult when we filter our relationships and experiences through the unstable emotions of the soul. Unfortunately, our physical bodies will respond according to what our emotions are telling us. But when a person gives his life over to God, his or her spirit comes alive. After presenting our soul (mind, will and emotions) to God, we will begin to move in the direction of His design, which unleashes new thoughts, His creativity and amazing adventures.

Think about it this way. God is spirit and man was created in God's image. However, our spirit experienced early death due to Adam's decision to follow Satan's suggestion rather than God's directive in the Garden of Eden. It is through Christ Jesus that our spirits are made alive again.

Our decision to submit to God through Christ's sacrifice on the cross enables us to reconnect with God and His adventurous life. How can I say that the creator of heaven and earth is adventurous? Just take a look around and consider the creativity involved in His creation. God knows how everything works. The grandeur and brilliance that emanates from the complex nature of His creation—that's how I know God is adventurous.

We are containers for God's creativity, which means God's potential is in us. Can you wrap your mind around the concept that God created us for His enjoyment? I believe God finds joy in our pursuit of His adventures—the ones we dream about, the ones He has already prepared for us. I will go on to say that for us to exist in mere survival mode is displeasing and contrary to God's original intent.

Jesus is quoted in John 10:10 saying, *The thief comes only to steal and kill and destroy; I have come that they may have life, and have it to the full.* You were not created to live a meager existence. Dream big dreams. Allow yourself to be an adventurous thinker. Try new things. Begin taking strategic risks.

Although pioneers face the greatest adversities when making new paths, they're the ones we remember. Nobody ever talks about the people who took the comfortable, previously established path. See yourself as a pioneer carving an exciting path to a life with no regrets.

WORDS OF WISDOM

To live a life with no regrets, you must be willing to live one accomplishment, one opportunity, one challenge, one calculated risk, and one adventure at a time.

DISCUSSION QUESTIONS

3.1. Do you have someone in your life who exemplifies adventure? If so, what does this person do that specifically demonstrates his/her zest for audacious living?

3.2. Have you ever been a dream killer or had a dream killer influence you?

3.3. What is on your bucket list?

3.4. Describe what you think an abundant life looks and feels like as it applies to you personally.

CHAPTER FOUR

GO WHERE THE ACTION IS

We make a living by what we get, but we make a life by what we give.
—Winston Churchill

Our Design
Do you think God designed us for boring, stale, predictable lives? I hope not.

Take a look at how we were created. Every part of our body, every limb, every organ, everything about us was designed to play, work, reach, hold, touch, point, run, jump, embrace, and so much more. Each specialized cell in our body is active, moving, shifting, all of them working together to keep us alive. Our blood flows through miles of veins and arteries, pumped by our continuously beating heart. God knows we are complex and unique human beings because He made us this way.

Think about it. We're given vision to see, hearing to distinguish sounds, taste buds and a sense of smell to enjoy food, and skin to feel marvelous sensations. And let's not forget, we have a mind and a mouth, so we can speak what's on our minds. We have been meticulously crafted. As human beings, we make known our creator's unlimited excellence.

But it's up to every individual to decide how he or she will use what he or she has been given. To what extent we respect our physical bodies is left up to us to decide. How we speak and what we choose to say is determined by the knowledge we've acquired. Likewise, what we hear and how we listen is filtered through our life experiences. Life is full of choices.

I've heard it said that the average person only uses about 10 percent of his or her brain capacity. That tells me there's a whole lot of potential left inside this head of mine. I understand that I was designed with a propensity to explore and examine, to engage and excel.

For example, as I write this, I'm sitting in the warmth and comfort of a mountain cabin in North Carolina overlooking a ski resort. My family and I come here every year during our Christmas break. From where I'm sitting, I can see people skiing, snowboarding and using inner tubes to squeeze out maximum fun from the slopes. Every once in a while, I look up from my keyboard and see my five-year old grandson trying to master his snowboard skills. I can't help but notice that as soon as he starts to slide down the hill, he looks up at me.

He sees me sitting behind the large glass window in the comfort of our cabin and waves his arms as if to say, "Come on Pop Pop! You're missing all the fun!"

I think to myself, how does he know what I'd be missing or what I would consider fun? I'm a man of many experiences and adventures, but he couldn't possible know how many times I've fallen while trying to conquer snowboarding. At my age, falling isn't all that much fun. Still, it's my job as a grandfather to put on my snowboard boots, strap on a snowboard and enjoy the next few hours with my grandson. My mission is to help him succeed, perhaps by showing him what *not* to do.

Yes, I fell down and over, and I did it a lot. But to see the joy those falls brought to the heart of my young grandson made me realize I did not have any regrets with regard to my decision to participate. I might have had regrets had I not given up some writing time to share a slippery, snowy adventure with my little buddy.

Whether you recognize it or not, your uniquely designed body and your mostly untapped mind craves that wind-in-the-face-going-so-fast-you-can-hardly-stand-it excitement. We can't (or we shouldn't) sit in the cabin and watch people enjoy life. Even though you might fall, make a wrong turn, smack your head on a tree branch, or worse yet, do a face plant into the trunk of a small tree, you can't let fear paralyze you. You have to leave your comfortable environment and go where the action is.

If you think about it, you can probably recall individuals, friends and family who have experienced grand failures. I'll bet many of them didn't give up on their dreams. In fact, I'm confident many people you know have failed but kept on trying, over and over again. It's the excitement of trying, the exhilaration of taking risks, and the anticipation of success that keeps people moving forward in life.

Audacious Friends

Earlier I mentioned the value of audacious prayers. What about the value of audacious friends? There's something very special about friends. They influence us. Friends become our loudest cheerleaders, greatest encouragers and biggest fans. This is the reason we must put ourselves in the presence of friends who can both inspire and motivate us.

Over the years I've learned that the more adventurous friends I have, the more adventures I experience. If you have friends who are full of adventure, then may I suggest you tap into that side of them and go along for the ride? If that's not the case, may I suggest you find some audacious friends? Friends who have accomplished great things have the ability to embolden us to achieve great things. Look for those people and become friends with them, then do something you've never done before.

Ask yourself this, what's the very worst that can happen if I try something I've never done before? If the worst outcome you can imagine is doable, then I say go for it. "It" probably won't happen as you've imagined. What would happen if you left your cocoon of comfort and tried new things? The rewards might be so wonderful you'll thank yourself. Repeatedly.

Revisit old ambitions. Go for the job interview. Take an extreme vacation. Meet someone new. Make that phone call and ask her (or him) out on a date. Go for it! Go ahead and take chances. To get what you want or need, you have to take chances.

If life isn't all that exciting, then understand that excitement doesn't just happen on its own. You have to go where the action is and take necessary risks. Things may not always work out the way you intended, but then again, you might be surprised. It's certainly better to try new things than to spend your life wishing you had.

If you're not healthy enough to jump out of an airplane or onto a snowboard, then find something you can do. Don't let your physicality restrict you. The key is to do things to the best of your ability. Maybe it's time to pick up the pen and start writing. Maybe you could pick up the guitar you put away years ago and start playing. What about enrolling in that cooking class you've been putting off? Maybe it's time to get a new hairstyle or consider how you could freshen up your wardrobe. Perhaps you should revisit the idea of making that documentary film you've always wanted to produce. Maybe it's time to start that blog you've been thinking about.

Speaking of minds and muscles, most people view Professor Stephen Hawking as one of the world's greatest minds, comparing him to Einstein. While I don't agree with his conclusions or theories, I have to admit he has challenged and changed the way we think about people with disabilities. Despite his limited ability to move and communicate, Hawking has married twice, fathered three children, authored books, and serves as the Director of Research at the Centre for Theoretical Cosmology at England's University of Cambridge.

Although Hawking's intellect is indeed amazing, his determination is even more astounding. He refuses to view himself as inadequate. Stephen Hawking recognizes each day might be his last, so he chooses to make the most out of each and every minute. Now that, my friends, is audacious!

Keep in mind that adventures begin right where you are. You must make a move.

Even if it's a small movement, move.

Immediate Change

There's an account in the Bible of a tax collector named Zacchaeus. He had a very powerful job yet was considered the lowest of men in his community. People looked down on him because of his wealth, which he obtained through dishonest means. When he heard that Jesus of Nazareth was passing through his town, he desperately wanted to catch a glimpse of the admired healer. In order to do so, he had to climb up a tree to see beyond the crowd. Apparently, Jesus noticed his extreme determination.

Luke 19: 5-6 says, *When Jesus reached the spot, he looked up and said to him, 'Zacchaeus, come down immediately. I must stay at your house today.' So he* (Zacchaeus) *came down at once and welcomed him* (Jesus) *gladly.*

Zacchaeus was inspired by Jesus' invitation and made a choice that changed his life. He went with Jesus to his house even though he could have stayed in the tree and watched events unfold as Jesus passed by. If he had continued to stay comfortable in his status quo, he would have missed the adventures Jesus had prepared for him.

Zacchaeus' perspective changed dramatically, so much so that he immediately decided to make radical amends. In Luke 19, verse 8 says, *But Zacchaeus stood up and said to the Lord, 'Look, Lord! Here and now I give half of my possessions to the poor, and if I have cheated anybody out of anything, I will pay back four times the amount.'*

What an incredible transformation! Zacchaeus took one step of faith and stepped out of his stale past life and into a powerful new life with Jesus. Even though his view from the tree was good, it wasn't nearly as productive as following Jesus.

But wait, there's more! In verse 9, Jesus tells Zacchaeus, *'Today salvation has come to this house, because this man, too, is a son of Abraham. For the Son of Man came to seek and to save what was lost.'* Notice Jesus did not say, "For the Son of Man has come to seek and to save **them** (or **those**) who were lost." He said, "**what** was lost." What does the "what" refer to?

Often misquoted or misinterpreted, this passage of scripture refers to the authority Adam gave up and the spiritual death mankind experienced as a result of disregarding God's commandment in the Garden of Eden. Genesis 2:16 says, *And the LORD God commanded the man, 'You are free to eat from any tree in the garden; but you must not eat from the tree of knowledge of good and evil, for when you eat of it, you will surely die.'*

Jesus' statement revealed His ability and intent to restore God's plan for mankind. Meeting Zacchaeus was the impetus for this important announcement. Would God have used someone else had Zacchaeus stayed up in the tree? Certainly. But I kind of like that God used a short mobster to declare His power and plan to rescue mankind from Adam's blunder. It was a pretty huge deal, don't you think? I do.

Zacchaeus found out happiness goes beyond having a large bank account and powerful job. He discovered that, by following the ways of Christ, he could experience what he had been missing in life. Zacchaeus found true joy and happiness when he accepted Christ's invitation.

Generosity

When we're involved in a new adventure, or we realize something we've experienced has altered our lives, don't we tend to want to share our happiness with as many people as possible? Sharing happiness and success with others releases a spirit of generosity, which can be very contagious. Someone once told me, "Putting in forty hours is how you make a living, but generosity is how you make a life." I take that to mean real life begins when you give yourself away. And it's true.

In fact, a crucial component to living a life with no regrets involves being generous with your time, talents, and treasures. I tell people to allow the radical change they've experienced to become the catalyst for a generous lifestyle. Be generous with family, friends, and those less fortunate. Volunteer in your community or church. Give generously when you find a charity or church that you know positively affects the lives of others. Make tithing to your local church a priority. If you don't have a home church, then give 10% of what you earn to charity. Why? Because the Bible says that "the tithe belongs to the Lord." Leviticus 27:30 says, *A tithe of everything from the land, whether grain from the soil or fruit from the trees, belongs to the LORD; it is holy to the LORD.*

Your bank account doesn't have to be the only means for unleashing blessings. Be generous with your talents. Again, your local church is a great place to donate whether your talent is singing, dancing, drawing, or organizing. If you're a talented tradesman, consider donating your time and tools to the church building project, homeless shelter, humane society, or nursing home. If you're a gifted teacher, consider teaching classes at a prison.

Please don't hoard your gifts and talents. Don't even think about letting them remain dormant. Why? Because the possibilities are endless and the rewards are heavenly.

WORDS OF WISDOM

Adventures begin right where you are, but you must make a move. Even if your movement seems insignificant, you are making progress.

Today is a good day to stretch your mind as well as your muscles.

DISCUSSION QUESTIONS

4.1. Describe the last time you felt an adrenaline rush while doing something unusual or exciting. Did you enjoy it? If so, what did you like about it? If not, what didn't you like about it?

4.2. Have you ever experienced failure in a big way? If so, how did it affect you?

4.3. Describe your most adventurous friend(s). What do you admire about them?

4.4. Has anyone ever called you generous? If so, were they referring to how you share your time, talents, and/or treasures?

CHAPTER FIVE

LEARN TO FORGIVE

Then Peter came to Jesus and asked, 'Lord how many times shall I forgive my brother when he sins against me? Up to seven times?' Jesus answered, 'I tell you, not seven times, but seventy-seven times.' Matthew 18:21-22

Forgive to Live
High school can be tough territory. As I recall my days as a student at Appling County High School, there was this one cold rainy day that left an impression on me and at least one other guy. Because of the weather students were allowed to wait in the hallways before school officially began. The morning hustle and bustle of arrival had been confined to the indoor hallways. Like many other students before him, John came running through the double doors to get out of the cold damp rain. He had to run by a group of thirty students, one of whom thought it would be funny to trip him while slapping his books out of his arms. John landed spread eagle, face down on the hard floor, books flying everywhere.

Laughter erupted up and down the hallway. I stood by and watched as John began pulling himself together, reaching for his broken glasses. He looked up to figure out his next move. I saw a tear roll down his face as he struggled to put his damaged glasses back on and rise from the slick floor.

All my life I've rooted for the underdog. My heart breaks immediately when I see someone being treated like an outcast. In every school and in every community, there are outcasts, and in our school, John was the epitome of nerd-dom. Besides wearing extra thick, horn-rimmed eyeglasses, he also wore his pants pulled up high, almost to his chest. He came to school in business attire short-sleeved, button down shirts, complete with a pocket protector filled with every writing utensil imaginable. It's a wonder he didn't carry a briefcase. He held his books close to his chest and walked with the pace of a frightened old man and the suspicious eyes of a betrayed old woman. Any attempt to have a conversation with him was awkward.

John didn't appear to have friends. I had to intervene. I helped gather John's books and get him up off the damp floor. I could see the embarrassment and humiliation on his face as the laughter continued. Together, John and I walked to his classroom. Before leaving, I asked, "Are you going to be okay?" He replied that he would. But I wasn't sure and I wasn't finished defending this guy. "Can I have your phone number? I'd like to give you a call sometime."

John looked surprised. He was unaccustomed to someone asking him for his phone number. I gave him a call that same afternoon. Apparently, this act of kindness had an effect on him because he began to follow me around like a lost puppy.

A few of my friends and I started to hang out with John. He was a nice kid.

Then one night I got a phone call from him. "That day you helped me, it was a pretty bad day. When I got home, I walked into my dad's bedroom, opened his nightstand and pulled out his revolver," he said. "I was preparing to take my own life when the phone rang."

Wow! While John was sitting on the side of his bed contemplating how to commit suicide with as little pain as possible, I had picked up the phone and made a call that literally saved his life.

"Eddie, had you not called me when you did, I would have taken my life," he admitted.

I knew John was damaged but at the time I couldn't fully grasp the depth of his pain or the intensity of his suffering. I was part of a divine interruption in the life of this young man, that much I recognized. I thanked God that everything fell into place at just the right time for John. I was very grateful John chose life over death.

Fast forward thirty years. My wife and I were in my hometown browsing through a couple of the shops when I saw a familiar face. Although we had aged, I could tell the years had not been kind to this fellow. His face was pale, showing signs of an awful sickness. He was extremely thin. Our eyes met at what seemed to be the exact same moment. "John?"

"Eddie?"

We shook hands and then I embraced him. "John, give me a big ol' hug, man. It's so good to see you!"

His naturally skeptical frown and leathery expression slipped into a slight smile. We talked for a while about our lives, sharing the things we'd been through, the jobs we held, and other everyday things. He told me about the three women he had married and divorced and his one daughter who he said didn't want much to do with him. He spoke of the ailments he had to deal with on a daily basis. He talked about his battle with cancer. The way he told it, it sounded like John had embraced his many health issues as if sickness had become some kind of unwanted but steadfast companion.

The pain, hurts and disappointments kept pouring out of him. Then out of nowhere he asked if I remembered that rainy day in high school. I told him I did. What he said next pretty much put everything into perspective. Suddenly, a scowl gripped his face and with teeth gritted, he said, "If I could go back to that day when I had a gun in my hand, I would put a bullet in someone's head."

It had been a long time since I had seen such a look of anger and desperation at the same time. John's venomous statement brought with it a moment of clarity. Bitterness had overtaken the last thirty years of his life, and that was why this forty-five year old man looked like he was sixty-five. John had not forgiven or forgotten the damage done to him. He kept his emotions buried for so long that a root of bitterness had grown deep in his heart and mind. Clearly, his lack of forgiveness contained an element of unexpressed rage, which was more fury than I wanted to imagine.

Why am I telling you this story? Because you will never live a life with no regrets as long as you hold on to offenses. The unhealthy grip of unforgiveness can and will ruin your life.

Forgiveness is a prominent theme in the Bible for good reason. Yet, the act of forgiving doesn't come easy for most of us. Our natural instinct is to recoil in self-protection and preservation when we've been injured or offended. It's not natural for us to let mercy, grace and understanding flow when we've been wronged. But forgiveness is a conscious choice, one my buddy John did not make.

The day my wife and I reconnected with John I felt compelled to try and redirect his thinking. "John, you've got to let that go. Have you ever thought that the person you're holding captive in your mind is really holding you captive to your past? Don't let your past imprison and enslave you. Let it go, man," I pleaded. "You've got to let it go."

What John didn't realize is that the bully most likely never gave the incident another moment's thought. He and all his friends probably forgot all about it. They were teenagers making stupid attempts to impress each other. The problem is John relived the humiliation nearly every day of his life for thirty years. And like a jackhammer, these thoughts continued to chip away at John's health, affecting both his strength and his sanity.

Bitterness is the vice that causes us to remember offenses so they will linger in our minds causing us to fume and seek out opportunities for revenge. Hebrews 12:14-16 says, *Make every effort to live in peace with all men and to be holy; without holiness no one will see the Lord. See to it that no one misses the grace of God and that no bitter root grows up to cause trouble and defile many.*

Our enemy, Satan, wants us to live with unforgiveness. God does not. Satan is delighted when unforgiveness consumes us and forms a destructive root of bitterness in our hearts. When we look for flaws in others, when we promote failure in hopes our offenders will suffer, when we let unforgiveness poison our thoughts, we are giving the enemy exactly what he wants. The enemy's plan is that we live unhealthy lives separated from God and others. Do I even need to say it? God's plan is the exact opposite.

Real Questions

Someone once said when you forgive, you don't change the past but you sure do change the future. Forgiveness is a promise, not a feeling. When you forgive others, you're making a promise never to use their past sins against them. Forgiveness is a choice, a willful act, not a feeling accompanied by an emotion. I believe forgiveness is a decision of our wills motivated by our obedience to God and His command to forgive. The Bible instructs us to forgive as the Lord forgives us. Colossians 3:13 says, *Bear with each other and forgive whatever grievances you may have against one another. Forgive as the Lord forgave you.*

But the real question is, how do we forgive when we don't feel like forgiving? How we do translate the decision and desire to forgive into a genuine change of heart? Since forgiveness goes against our human nature, we must forgive by faith and trust God to do a work in us until genuine forgiveness prevails. Trust God and His process. God honors our commitment to obey Him when we choose to forgive. He completes the work in His time. We must continue to forgive (our job) until the work of forgiveness (His job) is done in our hearts.

How will we know if we've truly forgiven someone? One writer penned these words, "When you release the wrongdoer from the wrong, you cut the malignant tumor out of your inner life. You set a prisoner free, but you discover that the real prisoner was yourself." We are the ones who suffer the most when we hold on to offenses. When we forgive, the Lord sets our hearts free from the anger, resentment and hurt. We will know when the work of forgiveness is done when we experience that freedom.

I don't think the old adage "forgive and forget" came from someone who experienced extreme emotional hurt. While forgetting can be healthy in that we've learned not to linger on the offense, sometimes forgetting can be impossible, and there's a reason for that. Human emotions can be so powerfully intertwined within our hearts and minds that holding on to an offense can damage us physically as well as emotionally. The heart is where our emotions take a seat and the reason revenge grows harmful roots in our hearts.

Unforgiveness has the potential to steal the very life out of you. Holding on to offenses creates stress, which causes anxiety that will eventually produce fatigue. When your body has to deal with fatigue, your heart rate is affected as blood flow is hindered. Other physical ailments begin to surface. Compounded physical ailments can lead to chronic health problems, even disease. This is why unforgiveness isn't something you play around with. It's something you deal with and cut out of your life.

Remember, all of this evil springs up the one moment you let something or someone offend you. My best advice is to deal with it from the start. It *is* possible to never let the offense take root.

Ephesians 4: 26-27 says it this way: *In your anger, do not sin. Do not let the sun go down while you are still angry, and do not give the devil a foothold.*

When we make room for thoughtful conversation on any matter that could potentially turn toxic, we're making room for a healthy future. Your future is too valuable to be delayed or destroyed by unforgiveness, especially when dealing with an offense can be as simple as saying, "Hold on a minute. Let's talk this through. I don't want to become offended in any way, nor do I want you to feel hurt. If we let this fester, our relationship, and possibly our health, will be affected."

We must recognize that forgiveness enhances our capacity for a productive and functional future. Forgiveness isn't easy but it *is* a necessary ingredient to living a life with no regrets.

Reasons to Forgive

"Why should I forgive when I've been hurt so badly?" you might ask.

One of the best reasons is because Jesus commanded us to do so. Matthew 6:14-16 says, *For if you forgive men when they sin against you, your heavenly Father will also forgive you. But if you do not forgive men their sins, your Father will not forgive your sins.* Forgiveness releases us from a spirit of judgment, and as we all know, that spirit does more harm than good.

Have you asked yourself this question: If God did not withhold His forgiveness from me, why should I be permitted to withhold forgiveness toward others? In Luke 6, verse 37 says, *Do not judge, and you will not be judged. Do not condemn, and you will not be condemned. Forgive, and you will be forgiven.*

Another important reason we should forgive is so that our prayers will not be hindered. Mark 11:25 says, *And when you stand praying, if you hold anything against anyone, forgive him, so that your Father in heaven may forgive you your sins.* That's a big one.

I've learned that prayer is the best way to break down any stubborn walls of unforgiveness. When I pray for someone who has mistreated me, God gives me a new set of eyes and I can't continue despising them. As I pray, I begin to see them as God sees them. Inevitably, compassion fills my heart. Everyone is God's beloved. I also see myself in a new light. I'm just as guilty of sin and failure as the next guy, which tells me I, too, am in need of forgiveness.

In short, we forgive out of obedience to the Lord but we must understand and remember that this command was given for our own good. It's our choice to forgive or conversely, not to forgive. Forgiveness is a decision we make, and when we decide to forgive, freedom is our reward.

WORDS OF WISDOM

Forgive us our trespasses, as we forgive those that trespass against us.
—The Lord's Prayer

DISCUSSION QUESTIONS

5.1. Are you someone, or do you know someone, whose physical and emotional life has deteriorated because of unforgiveness?

5.2. Do you believe unforgiveness prevents God from hearing our prayers?

5.3. Think about a time when unforgiveness poisoned your thoughts and held you prisoner. How long did you hold onto this particular offense before you decided to let it go?

5.4. If you haven't been able to extend forgiveness towards someone, what are your reasons for not pardoning them?

CHAPTER SIX

EMBRACE YOUR PAST

A man must be big enough to admit his mistakes, smart enough to profit from them, and strong enough to correct them.

—John C. Maxwell

So What?

Life is a roller coaster of peaks and valleys, trials and triumphs, so what? Here's what. We must give our experiences the opportunity to strengthen us.

The future is too important for you to allow the past to hold you captive. Putting your past behind you means learning to love yourself as you are. I'm not suggesting you forget your past. I'm saying don't live in the past. Why? Because our past failures and difficulties tend to steal love and confidence from us.

I hope you know God's love for us never decreases. Likewise, our love for ourselves shouldn't falter when we experience a setback. We need to have patience toward ourselves. A little benevolence will go a long way as we move forward and face life's challenges.

Take for example the Bible story of the great and mighty Samson who was betrayed by his trusted companion, Delilah. It's one thing to have an archenemy destroy you but it's another thing to be betrayed by a beloved friend. An archenemy is driven by hatred for you, which is why his evil plans and strategies should come as no surprise. What sends us reeling is when a trusted friend knocks the wind out of us with one simple act of betrayal.

Imagine with me, in the bowels of a cold, dark dungeon, we hear muffled sounds of human despair. In a mostly secluded corner, we see what appears to be the outline of a man curled up in the fetal position. This man seems out of place. His noticeably masculine stature, bulging muscles, partial beard and considerable size could have us believing he was Adonis if it weren't for the situation and awful prison stench.

A dusty beam of sunlight finds its way through the iron bars. Upon closer inspection, we see that the man's face is ominously illuminated. This is no ordinary man. His eye sockets are empty, yet we know this man was not born blind. It's plain for us to see that his eyes have been ruthlessly taken from him. And then we can't help but wonder, How could this mountain of a man be locked away in this disgusting dungeon?

The answer is, his girlfriend put him there. After much nagging from Delilah, Samson caved in and disclosed the secret to his extraordinary strength. He trusted Delilah (his friend, confidant and lover) not to reveal his secret, yet she told Samson's enemies all about it so they could subdue him.

She did it for money. All of Samson's previous victories were quickly overshadowed in one fleeting moment of indiscretion. Samson lost everything.

Judges 16:17 says, *So he told her everything. "No razor has ever been used on my head," he said, "because I have been a Nazirite set apart to God from birth. If my head were shaved, my strength would leave me, and I would become as weak as any other man."*

Back in the dungeon, we understand the depth of Samson's anguish. His groans reveal the chill of broken dreams and a future lost. Betrayal is a terrible word and a familiar story. Songs have been written, movies made and sermons preached about it. I'm sure most of us have experienced betrayal at one time or another.

In Chapter One, I shared a little about my experience of leaving the denomination I had been a part of for forty-six years. As my family and I proceeded to follow God's directive for our lives, we discovered some of our closest friends and acquaintances were okay with stabbing us in the back. So often that is the case. Those who are closest to us, and the ones we love the most, are the people who have the ability to hurt us the most, and quite often do. We uncovered lies, rumors, gossip and unfounded accusations, which I have to admit I wasn't expecting from our local church body of Christ-followers. Absolutely, we felt betrayed. However, I learned many years ago that Satan is the accuser of the brethren. I remind myself to always consider the source of any accusation. The Bible teaches us that we will be judged according to how we judge others, so I am very careful about judging or accusing others.

You cannot change how people treat you, but you can do something about how you respond. Throughout our ordeal, we were able to trust God and watch as He continued to work everything out, even while we were hurting. The key for us has always been to pursue God's purpose with excellence so that future generations can live a life with no regrets. We're never going to give away our destiny with God to the devices of the enemy. No way!

Go Out with a Bang

Even though at the end, Samson was not the man he once was, he didn't let his painful existence and his enemies' constant ridicule define him. He made a life-altering decision that, even though it would end his life, he would go out with a bang.

In a final act of faith, Samson asked God to allow him one last victory. He was determined to leave this life with no regrets.

The Bible says in Judges 16:28-30, *Then Samson prayed to the LORD, saying, "O Sovereign God, remember me. O God, please strengthen me just once more, and let me with one blow get revenge on the Philistines for my two eyes." Then Samson reached toward the two central pillars on which the temple stood. Bracing himself against them, his right hand on the one and his left hand on the other, Samson said, "Let me die with the Philistines!" Then he pushed with all his might, and down came the temple on the rulers and all the people in it. Thus he killed many more when he died than while he lived."*

Samson decided to leave it all on the field, placing everything in God's hands, even at the cost of his own life. If you think he had nothing to lose, I would have to disagree. The well-being and lives of generations to come were at stake. He put everything on the line to save the future nation of Israel from the terror of the Philistines.

The thought occurred to me that if there were a radio near Samson's prison cell, and Pink's hit song *Try* came on, he would have listened to and identified with the song's lyrics. I find Pink's message compelling.

> *Where there is desire, there is gonna be a flame.*
> *Where there is a flame, someone's bound to get burned.*
> *But just because it burns, doesn't mean you're gonna die.*
> *You gotta get up and try, try, try...*

If we could interview Samson, I'm sure he would say he wouldn't have had it any other way. I believe he was satisfied with his decision to go out giving it one more shot, one last try. I also think he would tell us that he gave it his all so that his children and grandchildren and their children's children could have the faith they would need to succeed against their enemies. Then, in my mind, he'd break into song, choosing the tune of his time that most resembled Pink's song, *Try*.

Repent and Move Forward

I have found that the word repent is often misused in Christian circles. It is frequently defined as the act of confessing sins, which is incorrect. Repentance isn't done with the mouth. It's done with the heart and mind. Your mind gives you the capacity to think and make decisions while your heart is linked to your motives. Your mind **knows** while your heart **feels**.

To repent is to change one's mind, or to turn around, change directions. The desire to change comes from your "knower." Motives are redirected in the heart. You can't keep doing the same thing over and over again and expect things to change. If something isn't working for you, stop doing it. If the path you're on is producing unwanted results, then choose a different direction. This is what repentance is all about—changing your mind and going in a different direction. And yes, it's appropriate to tell God about your change of heart. After all, God not only wants you to get on the right path, He also wants you to prosper along the way.

So you messed up. So what? Get up and try, try, try again! It's okay to make mistakes. Just be sure to learn from them. Repent (O God, remember me…), forgive yourself and move on. Don't blame others for your mistakes. Pick yourself up and reevaluate, then brush off any residue so you can go forward and live with no regrets.

Never let your enemies convince you that your past is unbecoming of God's blessings. Instead, remind the enemy that your future has been designed by God and is intended for His pleasure. Tell him that your past, mistakes and all, have worked together for good. Tell him that you can and will make a difference in this world because God created you to be an influential player. Declare out loud, "This is the day the Lord has made, I will rejoice and be glad in it!"

I can guarantee that someone on the planet needs to hear your story. You either know someone, or will meet someone who needs to know that it's possible to rise above the limiting beliefs our stories tend to produce. The truth is we are overcomers in Christ. God's word tells us in Hebrews 4:15-16, *For we do not have a high priest who is unable to sympathize with our weaknesses, but we have one who has been tempted in every way, just as we are–yet was without sin. Let us then approach the throne of grace with confidence, so that we may receive mercy and find grace to help us in our time of need.*

Destiny is calling and every day is a new beginning, so why not enjoy the journey?

WORDS OF WISDOM

Life should not be determined by a single event, whether good or bad. Life is a series of connected events designed to teach us important lessons and help us grow as individuals.

Remember, the future starts today, not tomorrow.

DISCUSSION QUESTIONS

6.1. Describe an experience you've had that strengthened you in a significant way.

6.2. Have you ever seen God work on your behalf as a result of your faith during a crisis? If so, how did God rescue or preserve you?

6.3. How would you define or explain the concept of repentance to a non-believer?

6.4. Do you believe there are people who need to hear your story? If so, could you identify them?

CHAPTER SEVEN

LEARN TO ELIMINATE

A man must be big enough to admit his mistakes, smart enough to profit from them, and strong enough to correct them.

—John C. Maxwell

Who are "They" Anyway?

God loves you too much to place your destiny in the hands of your critics. Your critics are mostly unaware of the work you've done or the scope of your aspirations. They have no vested interest in you or your project, yet they still have opinions. Take movie critics for an example. Though they had nothing to do with the making of the movie, they give films two thumbs up, or two thumbs down, or a certain number of stars by way of their personal opinions. Their declarations are just that—their opinions. The question is, do "they" matter?

First of all, who are "they" anyway? Critics are people who speak but offer no solid contribution when unsuspecting people give them an ear. Their intent is to keep the gossip going and the rumor mill turning. They can be faceless characters on the internet, or they can show up at your workplace, in your neighborhood, next to you at the hair salon, or even sit beside you at church. The truth is when you do something extraordinary you'll always bump into critics. Detractors are practically inescapable.

Even though critics have substantial opinions and a strange ability to sway others, you must ask yourself, should I allow this person to sway me away from my future? My dreams? My vision? Should "they" influence my destiny? Some critics have been described as haters, skeptics, or even jerks because they try to fight success. Whoever said "words will never harm you" probably wasn't in touch with the pain defamation causes. Words hurt. They can wound us deeply, but our response establishes a foundation for healing. A healthy response will always shorten the amount of time it takes to heal. Remember, it doesn't matter what your critics say or do. What matters is what you say and what you do.

When I was growing up, I spent many hours with an African American woman named Edna Mae. I remember running to her in tears because some kid (and sometimes my older brother) said mean things about me. She'd say, "If they ain't sayin' it right, don't listen." In other words, if what they're saying isn't true, then why are you listening? And if it's true, then wear the shoe.

I like to remind myself that people hear more than what is being said. In fact, people will use their imaginations to insert themselves and their ideas beyond the conversation. I've learned to listen properly. WHAT I hear is sometimes not as important as HOW I hear. What I hear is for the surface and speaks to the moment.

How I hear speaks to my heart and prepares me for my future. Again, if they ain't sayin' it right, I don't listen.

It's a pretty big deal to harm a person's character, but character assassins are out there. However, your good name will outlive their bad assessments and accusations. My mother always said, "If they're talking about you, at least they're giving someone else a break." That statement might not console us, but we can conclude that there must be some insecurity on the part of the critic.

I've discovered that there are two types of people who enter our lives. There are those who add and multiply, and those who subtract and divide. With that being said, it's up to you to say who stays and who gets eliminated. There are also two types of critics. They are:

1) Those who will intentionally offer constructive criticism and genuinely have your best interest in mind. These people deserve your time, your ear, and your heart.

2) Those who are determined to damage your reputation, put your character into question, and be nothing but an irritant. They have nothing constructive to offer, only destructive opinions. These people should be eliminated from your life.

I've prayed the following prayer for many years: *Lord, I pray that those who are supposed to be in my life will be brought by you in your timing and for your purpose...those who are supposed to be with me can't leave and those who aren't can't stay.*

Here's something else to take into account. Have you ever considered that critics might not be wrong about everything, just some things?

It might not be wise to automatically dismiss criticisms. Before letting feelings of being assaulted take over, you should evaluate their ideas to see if there is any truth to their disapproving comments. They might be in a position to shed light on a subject that those closest to us might not have been able to share. The things we avoid often are the things we tolerate. The things we tolerate are the things we will not change. If what "they" say causes us to look deeper, then we should review their remarks and consider what's what. Don't get offended. Listen with attentive repose, then eliminate the trash.

Here's something else we should take into consideration. Most people don't like to hurt anyone's feelings, so they use humor to convey their message and hope the hearer will understand the hidden meaning of what they're really saying. Never dismiss the funny quip, sarcastic jab or snide remark. If what has been said addresses a weakness, or uncovers a sore spot, make the adjustment and move on.

Don't Waste Your Time or Words

Don't waste your time becoming defensive when you come up against a dream stealer. Living with no regrets involves having a pure heart and clean hands. To lash out and waste time on people who don't matter is like casting your pearls before swine. You can defend your good name all day long but it won't change your critic's opinion. In fact, the more you lash out, the more ammunition you give them. They're hoping for a reaction so they can use it against you.

Many proverbs in the Bible address this issue of how to respond to critics. Here are a few that come to mind.

He who covers an offense promotes love, but whoever repeats the matter separates close friends. Proverbs 17:9

Even a fool is thought wise if he keeps silent, and discerning if he holds his tongue. Proverbs 17:28

Reckless words pierce like a sword, but the tongue of the wise brings healing. Proverbs 12:18

Criticism is a part of life and it doesn't matter how well you live your life, there will always be someone nearby who will find something to criticize. To avoid criticism, you must be prepared to do nothing, and I do mean nothing at all. Do anything and I'll guarantee you that you'll bump into a critic or two.

Let's take look at Job. He was a man the Lord called "perfect and upright" yet when calamity took over his life, his friends showed up willing to judge his situation. In their attempt to evaluate what Job had done wrong, they called him a hypocrite, a man of empty words, a mocker, and to top it off, they said he had a bad attitude. In the end, their judgment of Job was completely mistaken. They missed it by a mile. Yet Job's friends didn't waste any time criticizing and attacking Job's character. In essence, they were telling him that he was getting what he deserved.

On the other hand, Job was so in tune with God that he was the conversation of Heaven. In the first chapter of Job, verse 8 says, *Then the Lord said to Satan, "Have you considered my servant Job? There is no one like him on the earth; he is blameless and upright, a man who fears God and shuns evil."*

Now I'd have to say that is pretty righteous, yet Job's friends judged him at his lowest moment in life. Through it all, Job refused to turn away from God. As a result, Job was restored and blessed by God. In the final chapter of the book of Job, verse 12 says, *The Lord blessed the latter part of Job's life more than the first.*

I can say with 100% certainty that how you respond to critics determines the level of blessing God can trust you with in your next season of life. The remedy is to get a grip on your mouth and be careful to season your speech with the same mercy you would like someone to show you. We have the choice to speak life-affirming positive words or destructive negative words. If we don't learn how to properly deal with criticism, we become like our critics—inconsiderate.

People usually criticize others who have what they want, which is why your blessings stir up the critics, and like rabid dogs, they will attack any point of weakness they can find. But get this, what critics see as failure on your part, God uses to build your character. If you respond in anger and resentment, you can (and should) expect to reap anger and resentment. When you respond with grace and mercy, God will give you favor at the appropriate time in the appropriate manner.

Succeed Anyway

Never forget you've been designed for success and greatness is in you. Don't allow anyone who has no voice concerning your destiny to become a hindrance. Don't allow your mind to be filled with their toxic ideas or comments. At certain times, you may have more critics than supporters and more people talking behind your back than to your face; I say succeed anyway.

You can't please everyone and you'll never please the opponent, so identify those people, places and things that make you happy. Your happiness is predicated upon the people you choose to allow in your life. Notice I didn't say your joy is related to people, places and things. Happiness is temporal; joy is eternal. Specifically, the joy of the Lord is what remains when people, places and things change.

The Bible says in Nehemiah 8:10, "The joy of the Lord is your strength." Allow the Holy Spirit to give you wisdom to choose the people you should have in your life. Surround yourself with happy, positive people who share your values and goals. Those who have the same ethics and outlook will provide much needed encouragement as you strive to achieve goals, reach for your dreams and live a life with no regrets. These are the people who can lend a helping hand as you navigate through life's unforeseen obstacles. And also, should you need some, shall I say, fine-tuning, you can depend on these people to provide loving correction, which will be offered without a hidden agenda attached. Love these people.

Let me summarize with four simple steps to help you respond to criticism in a healthy manner.

Step one: Accept criticism. It's unavoidable.

Step two: Examine the source. Ask yourself, who is this coming from?

Step three: Decide not to take criticism personally. Be objective and try to learn from it. Ask yourself, is there any truth to what they're saying?

Step four: Commit the matter to the Lord and with His help you'll rise above it. Allow Him to defend you in His time, in His way.

Always remember that God loves you too much to place your destiny in the hands of your critics. Critics will spread their poison around until an infection occurs, so get them out of your system. Put them through the process of elimination and you will have no regrets!

WORDS OF WISDOM

If they ain't saying it right, don't listen.
—Edna Mae

DISCUSSION QUESTIONS

7.1. When you think of your critics, who comes to mind? Do you let their words affect you?

7.2. Has anyone ever used humor while trying give you advice? If so, did you understand their criticism? Do you think lighthearted sarcasm is okay to use when trying to help someone?

7.3. Has anyone ever offered to help you with something but there were strings attached? If so, how did you respond when you uncovered their hidden agenda?

7.4. Have you ever mentally and emotionally eliminated someone from your life?

CHAPTER EIGHT

MIND YOUR BUSINESS

Finally, brothers and sisters, whatever is true, whatever is noble, whatever is right, whatever is pure, whatever is lovely, whatever is admirable—if anything is excellent or praiseworthy—think about such things. Philippians 4:8

Daddy vs. Mrs. Busybody
Like many people, I grew up in a small town where everyone knew everyone and their business. My father, for many reasons, has always been extremely well respected in our hometown. For one, Daddy is a man of his word. For another, Daddy always minded his own business. You couldn't get him to entertain any form of gossip. My daddy is a genuinely honest man and is known as such. Presently, he's eighty-six years old and has hardly ever been sick a day in his life. Daddy still outworks my three older brothers and me. I would attribute his long life to honor and honesty.

Daddy has another noticeable virtue. He honors the spiritual and earthly authorities in his life. He has never once spoken a bad word to anyone about anyone at any time—that

I can remember. In every aspect of his life, in business and leisure, or while serving his family, friends, church or community, my daddy has always been honest in all matters, in every relationship. No one had to guess where he stood because his stance was already established in integrity.

Across the street from our house lived a lady I'll call Mrs. Busybody. Although she was extremely sweet (and incredibly loud due to a good bit of hearing loss), she enjoyed sharing community news. That was her term for gossip. I can remember, back when we still had house phones and Mrs. B. would call our house. You could hear her all the way in the other room, her phone voice carried that well.

If my mother answered the phone, Mrs. B. would tell her about her day, her ailments and slowly slip into the latest community news. My dear mother had a kindness about her wherein she allowed people to talk while she listened. But Mama didn't take Mrs. B. too seriously. She filtered each conversation and considered the source. Daddy, on the other hand, had a more practical approach to things. As long as I've known him (and I've known him all my life), Daddy always had a way of stopping negative things before they took root.

I remember one day Mrs. B. called to share the news about the latest pastoral change at our church. She knew all the details. She had the inside scoop on the new guy even though she had never met the man. And she knew every opinion of every member and all their reasons behind their misgivings. She even knew what would happen before the new pastor arrived. Actually, this was old news because she had already shared her views with several friends of my parents.

I can distinctly remember Daddy saying, "Now Mrs. B., I'm gonna go ahead and stop you now. Your gossip has preceded your phone call, and in all honesty, we love and appreciate you, but I just don't want to hear it." CLICK.

Too many people have a propensity for drama. If they're not watching soap operas, they're trying to live in one. The more drama they can experience, the more alive they feel. Wouldn't the world be a better place if more of us had the boldness to say, "I just don't want to hear it," or "I think I'll wait to hear this from the horse's mouth"? Or how about saying something like this, "My ears are not receptacles for your garbage. Let's all mind our own business."

In reality, if a busybody will talk *to* you about someone, he or she will talk *about* you to someone. In a letter to recent converts in Thessalonica, the apostle Paul and his companions gave plenty of practical instructions concerning godly living. The following verse addresses this topic specifically: *Make it your ambition to lead a quiet life, to mind your own business and to work with your hands, just as we told you, so that your daily life may win the respect of outsiders and so that you will not be dependent on anybody.* 1 Thessalonians 4:11

To become involved in someone's business without being invited is nothing more than an annoying intrusion. Plain and simple. I find that people who are unable to mind their own business are often dissatisfied with their own lives. Meddling in the affairs of others takes the focus away from their own dysfunctional lives. By putting the spotlight on others, they're less likely to deal with their own issues. Finding fault with others somehow makes them feel better. And since everyone has their own battles to fight and insecurities to handle, wouldn't those challenges be a whole lot easier to overcome if people weren't forcing unwarranted opinions into the situation? I say, definitely, yes!

Plus, people are too quick to judge other people's issues. Interestingly, these same people are not willing to look inside to examine their own issues. Here's how Jesus put it in Matthew 7, verses 4 and 5, *How can you say to your brother, 'Let me take the speck out of your eye,' when all the time there is a plank in your own eye? You hypocrite, first take the plank out of your own eye, and then you will see clearly to remove the speck from your brother's eye.*

I love how Jesus makes his position pretty clear concerning busybodies. He calls them hypocrites.

Don't get me wrong. Offering an occasional insight, or sharing an observation or two with a friend whose present situation appears to be stressful can be helpful. However, there's only so much advice that should be given and only so much advice that can be taken at one time. It's important to know your limits and your friend's boundaries. Don't abuse relationships. Even if you don't agree with what they're doing, you need to take a step back and let them make their own mistakes. In other words, if it doesn't concern you, or you don't have a personal invitation to share your thoughts, mind your own business.

Someone I consider to be my father in the faith told me never to take up a cause that isn't my own. He told me this time and again whenever I would try and defend someone I thought needed my help, when truthfully, it was none of my business. A life with no regrets is better obtained when we stop abandoning our own lives to delve into the lives of people who don't want our input anyway. Deal with you, work on you, build your character, stay calm, grow up and mind your own business.

And just so you know, busybodies are placed in the same category as murderers and thieves. 1 Peter 4:15 says, *If you suffer, it should not be as a murderer or thief or any other kind of criminal, or even as a meddler.* A person's true character will eventually reveal itself.

This is why you don't want to be a meddler or hang out with one. When you realize someone's impression of you will be determined by the words you speak, then you are in control of whether or not they think of you as a meddling gossip, or a leader, protector and friend. The Bible speaks directly to this issue. Proverbs 18:20-21 says, *From the fruit of his mouth a man's stomach is filled; with the harvest from his lips he is satisfied. The tongue has the power of life and death, and those who love it will eat its fruit.*

I'd like to add that it makes no sense to complain about what you permit. If you allow gossip to marinate in your mind, then the results are on you. Your circumstances are largely dependent upon what you authorize. The moment you make a decision that "enough" is enough, that's when things begin to change. Break free from busybodies, don't listen to gossip, and mind your own business. Have I said that enough?

WORDS OF WISDOM

The best way to deal with busybodies is to ignore them.

Give busybodies enough rope and they'll eventually hang themselves.

DISCUSSION QUESTIONS

8.1. Do you know a busybody? Does anyone think of you as a busybody? What is your definition of gossip?

8.2. Can you keep a secret when asked? Do you tell people secrets?

8.3. Have you ever been accused of giving unwanted or unasked for advice?

8.4. Have you ever taken up a cause that is not your own? If so, what were the consequences?

CHAPTER NINE

LEARN TO LAUGH

If you can laugh at it or laugh with it, you can live with it.

—Eddie Tomberlin

Merry Medicine

Laughter is good medicine no matter what's ailing you. Plain and simple, that's the truth. My granddaddy used to tell me to always smile because it leaves people guessing. I'd like to add something to his words. Smile because smiling is starter fluid for laughter.

Look around. If you're not surrounded by people who make you smile or laugh, then may I suggest you pick up the phone and call some friends who can and will make you laugh? Please don't hang around attention-seeking sad sacks. Your life is too valuable. You don't need it, you don't want it, and you can't afford it, and by "it" I mean Negative Nellies and their kind. Your life should be packed full with happy people.

Make way for laughter because life's too short to let the pessimists take over. I've never understood why so many people see only the worst in people and situations. Maybe it's because they've never looked inward and had a good laugh at their own mess. Take me, for example. I'm a complete mess when I think about the second day of my sophomore year in high school. If this story doesn't make you laugh, then you might be dead.

It was a warm, pleasant August morning, but I had one of those irritating end-of-summer head colds. I'm talking about the kind of cold where you must have a box of Kleenex close by within arm's reach. Ignoring the need for proper nutrition to fight off illness, my brother Robbie, my buddy Kent and I stopped by Hardee's for a big steak, egg and cheese biscuit. That morning I ate two of those wonderful breakfast sandwiches, more than I probably should have eaten, but oh, how I loved those hot-off-the-griddle breakfast treats before school.

Following our stop at Hardee's, I found myself in homeroom sitting next to a pretty girl named Lori. She was, or so I thought at the time, the prettiest girl in school. She was not only beautiful, she was also talented, super sweet and she smelled nice. I, on the other hand, was not looking so good. I was uncomfortable, tensing up from the pressure building up in my stomach. The problem was the two greasy sandwiches in my belly. They had made me gassy, and not a little gassy, a lot gassy.

I remember watching the clock, hoping the bell would ring so I could relieve myself of the horrendous pressure. It was 8:15, just five more minutes and I could take care of business. But something happened. Lori's pink hairbrush had made its way to the edge of her desk and was about to begin its descent to the dirty school floor—I couldn't let her hairbrush hit the floor, are you kidding? And that's when it happened. With tiger-like reflexes, I sprang toward the brush, reaching, stretching and bending. In my condition, bending was a huge mistake.

It was all so surreal. Everything went into slow motion as my heroics went from bad to worse. All the pressure created from those two wonderful biscuits came flying out of me with sounds only a large wild bull elephant could make. The terror, the embarrassment, the shame and the laughter—even sweet Lori couldn't contain herself. She, along with the rest of my classmates, thought my indigestion was very amusing. I thought it would be best if I joined in. However, I laughed so hard that a fine flow of mucus gushed out of my nose onto my shirt. Could things have gotten any worse?

As you can imagine, the hilarity quickly turned into disgust. I had repulsed everyone. *Think fast, Eddie! How do you get yourself out of this mess? Whatcha gonna do now?* Without missing a beat, I grabbed Lori's brush, jumped to my feet and shouted, "I saved it! Lori's hairbrush has been saved! Praise the Lord!" Jumping up and down in great jubilee and much to my surprise (and liking), the class began to cheer with me.

Why would I share this awkwardly nasty but funny story? I don't mean to offend anybody, but if you are offended, please chill out. Relax. Give me a break. Don't take this life or yourself too seriously. I included my breakfast biscuit story because I learned something that day. I learned how to laugh at myself. And this is why I'm often quoted as saying, "If you can laugh at it or with it, you can live with it."

You'll never run out of material if you're the subject of your amusement. When you learn to laugh at yourself, no matter what the situation, you automatically increase your lifespan as well as the quality of those years. This is what the Bible verse refers to when it says in Proverbs 17, verse 22, *A cheerful heart is good medicine, but a crushed spirit dries up the bones.* Many studies have shown that people who laugh often are healthier than those who don't.

Laughter tends to free the mind and clear away unwanted emotions. It is a powerful antidote to mental stress and physical pain. Nothing works faster or better in an unpleasant situation than bringing your mind and body back into balance with a good laugh. Humor inspires hope, which can lighten your burden and help you connect with others. With so much power to heal and renew, the ability to laugh is a tremendous resource God has made available to us. I recommend you use it often.

Let's examine this amazing concept even further. Here are just a few things I found while researching this subject.

1. Laughter relaxes the whole body, leaving muscles in a relaxed state for up to 45 minutes. A good hearty laugh (along with bending) relieves physical tension, as I've mentioned earlier.
2. Laughter boosts the immune system by decreasing stress hormones while increasing infection-fighting antibodies in our cells. Laughter helps our bodies resist disease.
3. Laughter triggers the release of endorphins, the body's natural feel-good hormones. Endorphins

promote an overall sense of well being and can temporarily relieve pain.
4. Laughter protects our hearts by improving the function of blood vessels and increasing blood flow. Laughing can help protect you from heart attacks and other cardiovascular problems.

Thinking of improving your health? Start by laughing. This might be the prescription our physicians should be handing out to their patients. *LAUGH!* Get a good belly laugh going and you're on the path to healing whatever's ailing you.

But wait, there's even more benefits to laughter. Having fun adds joy and zest to life, eases fear and anxiety, and stabilizes and improves moods, which allows us to be more resilient. When you purposely infuse merrymaking into your life, your relationships will improve. You'll attract others who love being around joyful people. This means your teammates, colleagues, friends, neighbors and family members will be more inclined to help you and less inclined to fight with you if you enter the room or a situation with a sense of humor. Have you ever noticed how your crazy aunt or uncle seems to live forever? There's a reason for that. They laugh a lot.

Life Should be Enjoyed, Not Tolerated

Life should be enjoyed, not tolerated. Grumpy, religious, stiff-necked people take heed. Craziness, silliness, humor, and everything that causes laughter or comes with it, adds to our vitality. A Spanish nun, Theresa of Avila, is quoted saying, "She who laughs, lasts." Historians tell us she would intentionally look for apprentices who knew how to laugh, eat and sleep. Sister Theresa believed that if the apprentice ate well, she was healthy. If she slept well, she would most likely be free of sin. And if they laughed, she had the necessary proclivity to survive a difficult life.

Remember that joy usually starts with a smile, followed by a chuckle, which can often turn into uncontrollable giggles, which may erupt into animated belly laughter. And that's a good thing. Someone said that love may make the world go 'round, but laughter keeps us from getting dizzy. Laughter is bound within the hearts of those who genuinely enjoy and appreciate life. The key is to enjoy life.

Give yourself plenty of reasons to smile. Take time to see the beauty around you. Learn to live in the moment and to cherish that moment. Take a walk along the seashore, go on a hike and smell the flowers, or watch the sun set or rise with the intent to develop (or redevelop) your childlike sense of wonder. Did you know that children laugh an average of four to five hundred times a day as compared to adults, who laugh only twelve to fifteen times a day?

It may be that you feel depressed, disconnected and joyless. Perhaps you've been burdened by stress and you're worried because you don't see any conceivable relief in your future. If that's you, then it's time to laugh. Some of you might have to practice the art of laughing by starting with a smile and letting yourself chuckle, snicker, or giggle, even if you have to fake it. Go ahead and LAUGH! Let it out! Laugh until you feel something release in you, just be careful what you release.

Here's an exercise for you: TRY TO MAKE SOMEONE ELSE LAUGH. Give yourself a reward when it happens if you like. It's okay to read from a joke book. The idea is to get the laughter started. I'm positive you'll like the results.

Ask God to Fill Your Heart

In our most trying, stressful moments we should ask God to fill our hearts with His joy. In Job chapter 8, verse 21 says, *He will yet fill your mouth with laughter and your lips with shouts of joy.* Likewise, Psalm 30:11-12 says, *You turned my wailing into dancing; removed my sackcloth and clothed me with joy, that my heart may sing to you and not be silent.* God has the perfect prescription for wholeness, and He will rework your heart if you let Him.

By now we all know life comes with unexpected twists and turns. Some moments are good, and some are not so good. Have you ever considered that life is a series of moments that establishes an event, and a series of events establishes a season, and seasons make up a life? If laughter can bring healing to a moment, then I believe laughter can infect every event and season, as well as an entire life. And let's not forget that a sense of humor will keep you grounded.

For example, one day my wife and I were having an intense conversation that quickly turned into an argument. During our disagreement, I couldn't get my words to form correctly. Nothing I said made any sense. I'm a fairly articulate person, and at this moment, I realized my sentences, my thoughts, my words were ridiculous. When LaDonna could no longer hold it in, she started to snicker, which made me even more frustrated, which produced even more jumbled sentences.

While I was speaking, darling LaDonna decided to quench her thirst. That was a mistake. She was unable to swallow her sip of tea because what I was saying caused her to laugh and spew. Suddenly everything was funny. We tried not to laugh because we were so infuriated with each other but it was too late. Our laughter became uncontrollable. We laughed right through our anger until we knew that to pick up our intense conversation wouldn't be worth the effort.

And that, my friends, is it for the Tomberlin blooper reel. I'm sure you have some bloopers of your own. Please feel free to share them so I can join in on the fun.

I'd like to add one final thought. If the day comes when I'm lying on my deathbed, I want to be surrounded by laughter. I want the grandchildren to crawl and sit all over my bed. I want my friends and family to talk about the fun adventures we've had together. I want the room to be filled with laughter.

Don't get me wrong. Tears will come later. When the coffin comes rolling by, they'd better be crying about how they can't live without me. They should be overcome with grief at my passing—I'm talking wailing, whooping and squalling. But when the commotion finally settles down, there had better be a preacher giving a magnificent eulogy, one to be remembered, perhaps for the centuries. I want to be sent off with more laughter than is appropriate for a funeral. I want to be missed, not forgotten, if you know what I mean.

Now, if you have to learn to laugh, then by all means, start practicing. If you don't laugh enough, then remember to laugh. If you're like me, a jolly person at heart, keep it up, and by all means, spread some of that good stuff around. Laughter is great medicine for what ails us all.

WORDS OF WISDOM
Life should be enjoyed, not tolerated.

DISCUSSION QUESTIONS

9.1. Do your friends make you laugh? Are you known for your sense of humor?

9.2. What makes you laugh? Create a list.

9.3. Can you recall a time when a sense of humor healed a stressful situation? Explain the circumstances.

CHAPTER TEN

LEARN TO DISCERN

Discernment is not a matter of simply telling the difference between right and wrong; rather it is telling the difference between right and almost right.

—Charles Spurgeon

Cleavers and Leavers

Too often regrets inhabit our human relationships. So many people, so many regrets. If that's your reality, you need to learn to discern others' motives and your reasons for having relationships. In the previous chapter, we discussed how important it is to stay away from busybodies, but how can we protect our interactions with people so as to guarantee a future with no regrets? The answer is to be selective.

It's okay to let someone go when the relationship has run its course. It's not about being cold-hearted, arrogant or conceited. It's about accepting the fact that not everyone deserves a place in our lives. Obviously, every relationship is important and complex, but it's important to remember in this age of Facebook, we don't have to be friends with everybody.

The story of Ruth in the Old Testament offers readers a good example of relational sensitivity. Ruth was a Moabite woman and the daughter-in-law of a Jewish woman named Naomi. The book of Ruth tells the story of how a severe famine drove Naomi's family from their homeland. Elimelech, his wife Naomi, and their two sons found a better life in the non-Jewish land of Moab, east of their home in Bethlehem.

Elimelech's sons married Moabite women, Orpah and Ruth. In time, Elimelech and his sons died, leaving Naomi to live with her daughters-in-law. Upon hearing that the famine was over, Naomi decided to return to her homeland and urged her daughters-in-law to return to their mothers in Moab. After much dispute, Orpah accepted Naomi's wishes and left, weeping. But Ruth "clung to" Naomi and uttered the now famous words: "Where you go I will go; where you lodge, I will lodge; your people shall be my people, and your God my God." (Ruth 1:16) These beautiful words are still used in wedding ceremonies and vows today.

Still, Naomi and Ruth had no money or men to take care of them. Upon their return to Bethlehem, Ruth went into the fields to gather whatever grain she could find. A landowner named Boaz saw Ruth gleaning and had a conversation with her. Boaz told Ruth that not only will his workers protect her, but they will also share provisions with her. Ruth thanked Boaz but questioned why she, a foreigner, should be the recipient of such kindness. Boaz replied that he had learned of Ruth's faithfulness to her mother-in-law, Naomi.

In Ruth 4, verses 11 and 12, *Boaz replied, 'I've been told all about what you have done for your mother-in-law since the death of your husband—how you left your father and mother and your homeland and came to live with a people you did not know before. May the Lord repay you for what you have done. May you be richly rewarded by the LORD, the God of Israel, under whose wings you have come to take refuge.'*

When Ruth told Naomi about Boaz, the generous landowner, the older widow was very pleased. The benevolent man was a kinsman of Elimelech, her late husband. This meant that Boaz had the opportunity to take Naomi and Ruth into his care as a kinsman-redeemer if and when a marriage took place. Naomi convinced her daughter-in-law to go to Boaz in the night to offer herself to him as a candidate for marriage. After negotiations concluded with another eligible kinsman, Boaz was able to marry Ruth and they had a son named Obed. Fortunately for Grandma Naomi, she was granted the opportunity to raise and care for this child who would grow up to be the grandfather of King David. Now that's a story about leavers and cleavers!

Throughout our lives, there will be those we can affectionately label leavers and those who can be called cleavers. Some will travel with us through a majority of our lives, and others will leave, exercising seasonal loyalty, if you will. Don't be too quick to judge a leaver. We can't know the full extent of what he or she is dealing with or who or what is influencing his or her decisions.

I've come to appreciate how God blesses our endeavors when we discard those things and people who can potentially keep us from realizing our destinies. Which means if you're looking to live a life with no regrets, you must keep in mind that there will always be leavers and cleavers. By learning to release people at the appropriate time in the appropriate manner, you'll discover how God replaces the leavers with other people who will assist you in your next season of life.

I refuse to spend my life motivating people to stay when, in reality, they should leave. I don't want my journey to be delayed unnecessarily. Sometimes God has me enter an extremely uncomfortable situation to shake free the "should-be leavers" in my life. Perhaps that's His way of moving me forward. God knows I don't want to go through life trying to fulfill His assignments with unwanted baggage. Let's face it. Some relationships create strife and tension that in the long run become detrimental to our futures.

Even though every person I meet matters a great deal to me, there are only a few individuals whom I expect will go through life right by my side. There are only three constants in my life, and I refuse to lose any one of them. They are my faith in God, my integrity and my family. Not everyone who starts with me will end with me, and that's okay. I'm cleaving to the ones God has chosen for me. My Heavenly Father, He knows best.

The Right Mixture

Making connections with new people exposes us to varying perspectives and greater ideas, which is why I believe God wants us to experience many relationships throughout our lifetime. However, finding the right mixture of associates, friends, and counselors still requires discernment. Figuring out who should stay and who should leave ought to involve the Holy Spirit. With God's help, you can find positive people who share your values. Sharing your dreams and visions with others can be intimidating, if not humiliating, so it's best to align yourself with people who can make healthy contributions.

Remember Ruth and Naomi? They traveled to a strange land only to lose the livelihood they were seeking. When the patriarch of the family and his sons died, Naomi, Orpah and Ruth had to modify their living arrangements. This resulted in new relationships, most notably for Ruth. Had she not been a woman of great character, she might not have clung to Naomi like she did. Had she not clung to Naomi like she did, the bloodline to King David would not have been the same, or at all! Now that's something to consider.

I realize some people enjoy the challenge and even have the ability to manage a multitude of friendships. By all means, if this is you, do what makes you happy. For me, I've come to appreciate the wonderful people who have entered my life and stayed a good long while. Some of these folks will be with me throughout my entire lifetime, and for them, I'm very grateful. And then there are those people who, although they've added great value to my life, for some reason or another, they're no longer around. I'm also very grateful for them. On the other hand, some people come and go rather quickly, and I truly appreciate their contributions as well. I continually thank the Lord for everyone who has entered, stayed or exited my life.

Whether relationships are for a season, a reason or a lifetime, it's important to use discernment in order to fully appreciate the purpose and usefulness of each relationship. As we progress toward our destinies, we should welcome people with open arms. In the same way, we should allow them to leave, with love and acceptance. People shouldn't feel pressure from us to stay, nor should we have an expectation of reward if they stay. The key is to have a thankful heart for each relationship you've enjoyed (or endured). Gratitude is the spark that helps us transition from one relationship to another.

WORDS OF WISDOM

Remember that when it comes to relationships: no pressure, no expectations, no regrets.

DISCUSSION QUESTIONS

10.1. Make a list of the people you know will be with you until the end.

10.2. Make another list of the people who have come into your life for a season or a reason.

10.3. Have you ever stayed in a relationship too long? If so, were you able to break free and move on?

CHAPTER ELEVEN

GOD'S WILL REVEALED

Sir, my concern is not whether God is on our side; my greatest concern is to be on God's side, for God is always right.

—Abraham Lincoln

Simplicity

This is a short chapter because one of the greatest problems in the Christian faith is that people tend to overanalyze and complicate a simple gospel. We hold on to the idea that God is so huge that there should be some deep revelation that will make our lives work, calling that God's will. Many of us have heard that God's thoughts and ways are much higher than ours, which is true, but when it comes to God's plan for redeeming mankind, His plan is not complicated.

Still, Christians ask a lot of questions, for example, what exactly is God's will for my life? How can I know what He wants me to do? How can I hear His voice? What are my instructions? Whom should I marry? Where should I work? What am I called to do? What ministry am I supposed to be in? We entertain the notion that if we're disobedient in any of these areas our lives will surely fall apart.

Let me ease your mind. If you have accepted God's plan for redemption through the finished work of Jesus, His death and resurrection, the ultimate and final sacrifice for sin, then you're smack dab in the center of God's will. Problems arise when we are duped into believing that God's will has something to do with where we work, who we marry, how many children we have, where we go, what church we attend, and so on. But God's will is much simpler than what we've unintentionally conjured up.

Let me illustrate how simple the gospel message is with a story. A college physics professor instructed his students to take out one piece of paper and told them to fill the sheet with all the information they thought they might need to pass his final exam. On exam day, the students filed into the classroom with their paper filled to the brim with notes, but only one student entered the room accompanied by a friend. He took out his sheet of paper and asked his friend, who happened to be a physics professor, to stand on it. This student consolidated all the information he would need to ace the exam by asking his friend to stand on a piece of paper. What everyone else spent all night preparing, this student did in a moment by simply asking his friend for a favor.

Do yourself a favor and ask God to forgive you and accept His plan. It's really that simple.

The Best News One Could Ever Hear

Some preachers overcomplicate the good news of Jesus Christ. The simple truth of this matter is this: God's will for us is to be saved, nothing more, nothing less. Our salvation is the full inheritance of His will. God's salvation tells us we have access to everything He has for us by the indwelling of His Holy Spirit. But to access everything He has for us demands growth in our knowledge of Him. The more we know, the more we grow in wisdom. And because life is filled with opportunities and options, it's important to use godly discernment to make right choices.

There is a verse in the Bible that states God's will plainly. It's found in 1 Timothy 2, verses 3-4: *This is good, and pleases God our Savior, who wants all men to be saved and to come to a knowledge of the truth.*

There's nothing more to be done except for us to believe and accept what God has already done. After that, we've become participants in God's will. Not only that, but we've become partakers in God's divine nature. 2 Peter 1:3-4 says, *His divine power has given us everything we need for life and godliness through our knowledge of him who called us by his own glory and goodness. Through these he has given us his very great and precious promises, so that through them you may participate in the divine nature and escape the corruption in the world caused by evil desires.*

Because we've accepted Christ Jesus, we've been blessed with every spiritual blessing needed to succeed in life. Nothing explains this better than the scripture verses found in Ephesians 1, starting with verse 3. *Praise be to the God and Father of our Lord Jesus Christ, who has blessed us in the heavenly realms with every spiritual blessing in Christ. For he chose us in him before the creation of the world to be holy and blameless in his sight. In love he predestined us to be adopted as his sons through Jesus Christ, in accordance with his pleasure and will.* The apostle Paul goes on to say, *In him we have redemption through his blood, the forgiveness of sins, in accordance with the riches of God's grace that he lavished on us with all wisdom and understanding.*

Did you get that? It's God's pleasure that we be forgiven and have enjoyment in this life. It's not just about what we'll experience someday when we get to heaven. It's about what we can enjoy now, right here in this crazy world.

In verse 9 Paul goes on to say, *And he made known to us the mystery of his will according to his good pleasure, which he purposed in Christ, to be put into effect when the times will have reached their fulfillment—to bring all things in heaven and on earth together under one head, even Christ.*

And here's the best part. Verses 11 through 13 adds, *In him we were also chosen, having been predestined according to the plan of him who works out everything in conformity with the purpose of his will, in order that we, who were the first to put our hope in Christ, might be for the praise of his glory. And you also were included in Christ when you heard the word of truth, the gospel of your salvation. Having believed, you were marked in him with a seal, the promised Holy Spirit, who is a deposit guaranteeing our inheritance until the redemption of those who are God's possession—to the praise of his glory.*

Christians have access to all of God's great and precious promises. We don't have to leave anything in the heavenly vault or on the table. Our mediator has delivered His end of the deal so we could have it all. It was His plan, His purpose and His will that we be included and sealed. We can't get any more assurance than that, and if you don't have access to all of God's promises, it's only because you haven't asked.

Let me be clear, God's will and intent for all of mankind has always been first, a relationship with Him, then and only then, dominion in the earth.

I have one last question for you. Have you considered the difference between God's purpose and His calling and assignments? God's unconditional love for us includes callings and assignments to fulfill, which are part of our daily employment in His Kingdom here on earth, but His will, our salvation, brings us into our inheritance immediately and will never cease. One doesn't depend on the other. Understand this principle, and you're well on your way to living a life with no regrets!

WORDS OF WISDOM

The world and its desires pass away, but the man who does the will of God lives forever. 1 John 2:18

DISCUSSION QUESTIONS

11.1. Have you ever been told that good works are required to get into heaven? How did this make you feel?

11.2. Have you accepted God's plan for salvation? If so, have you ever shared your testimony with others?

11.3. Do you struggle with knowing or understanding God's will for your life?

11.4. Do you feel that God has a calling upon your life? If so, can you describe your assignment?

11.5. Are you actively engaged in fulfilling God's calling for your life? If not, what is holding you back?

DISCUSSION QUESTIONS

CHAPTER ONE Challenge the Status Quo

1.1 Have you ever "left it all on the field" before? If so, describe the circumstances and your reasons.

1.2 What, if anything, are you holding back from God? What are you holding back from others, especially those with obvious needs?

1.3 What would it look like if you left it all on the field for your church or your family? What would change?

1.4 Recall a time when you challenged the status quo. How did you feel before, during and after? What might not have happened if you had played it safe?

CHAPTER TWO Learn to Explore

2.1. Have you ever felt safe, secure and miserable? If so, what were the circumstances?

2.2. Describe your religious upbringing. If you were not raised in a denominational church or religious family, did you ever have the inclination to explore religious studies?

2.3. If you were raised in a denominational church, did you ever question any of the church's teachings or values?

2.4. Describe a time when you prayed for direction and followed God's leading.

CHAPTER THREE Dream Again

3.1. Do you have someone in your life who exemplifies adventure? If so, what does this person do that specifically demonstrates his/ her zest for audacious living?

3.2. Have you ever been a dream killer or had a dream killer influence you?

3.3. What is on your bucket list?

3.4. Describe what you think an abundant life looks and feels like as it applies to you personally.

CHAPTER FOUR Go Where the Action Is

4.1. Describe the last time you felt an adrenaline rush while doing something unusual or exciting. Did you like it? Why, or why not?

4.2. Have you ever experienced failure in a big way? If so, how did it affect you?

4.3. Describe your most adventurous friend(s). What do you admire about them?

4.4. Has anyone ever called you generous? If so, were they referring to how you share your time, talents, and/or treasures?

CHAPTER FIVE Learn to Forgive

5.1. Are you someone, or do you know someone, whose physical and emotional life has deteriorated because of unforgiveness?

5.2. Do you believe unforgiveness prevents God from hearing our prayers?

5.3. Think about a time when unforgiveness poisoned your thoughts and held you prisoner. How long did you hold onto this particular offense before you decided to let it go?

5.4. If you haven't been able to extend forgiveness towards someone, what are your reasons for not pardoning them?

CHAPTER SIX Embrace Your Past

6.1. Describe an experience you've had that strengthened you in a significant way.

6.2. Have you ever seen God work on your behalf as a result of your faith during a crisis? If so, how did God rescue or preserve you?

6.3. How would you define or explain the concept of repentance to a non-believer?

6.4. Do you believe there are people on this planet who need to hear your story? If so, could you identify them?

CHAPTER SEVEN Learn to Eliminate

7.1. When you think of your critics, who comes to mind? Do you let their words affect you?

7.2. Has anyone ever used humor while trying give you advice? If so, did you understand their criticism? Do you think lighthearted sarcasm is okay to use when trying to help someone?

7.3. Has anyone ever offered to help you with something but there were strings attached? If so, how did you respond when you uncovered their hidden agenda?

7.4. Have you ever mentally and emotionally eliminated someone from your life?

CHAPTER EIGHT Mind Your Business

8.1. Do you know a busybody? Does anyone think of you as a busybody? What is your definition of gossip?

8.2. Can you keep a secret when asked? Do you tell people secrets?

8.3. Have you ever been accused of giving unwanted or unasked for advice?

8.4. Have you ever taken up a cause that is not your own? If so, what were the consequences?

CHAPTER NINE Learn to Laugh

9.1. Do your friends make you laugh? Are you known for your sense of humor?

9.2. What makes you laugh? Create a list.

9.3. Can you recall a time when a sense of humor healed a stressful situation? Explain the circumstances.

CHAPTER TEN Learn to Discern

10.1. Make a list of the people you know will be with you until the end.

10.2. Make another list of the people who have come into your life for a season or a reason.

10.3. Have you ever stayed in a relationship too long? If so, were you able to break free and move on?

CHAPTER ELEVEN God's Will Revealed

11.1. Have you ever been told that good works are required to get into heaven? How did this make you feel?

11.2. Have you accepted God's plan for salvation? If so, have you ever shared your testimony with others?

11.3. Do you struggle with knowing or understanding God's will for your life?

ABOUT THE AUTHOR

Eddie Tomberlin was born and raised in Baxley, Georgia, a small town he considers one of the state's finest and friendliest. Eddie has spent most of his youth and adult life involved in church ministry. Over the years he has been extremely successful serving as a music minister, youth pastor and senior pastor of both small and large congregations. He and his wife LaDonna are the founding pastors of a non-denominational ministry called Grace Culture located in Guyton, Georgia. The vision for Grace Culture is to be a place for anyone to belong. Eddie says, "We are simply a cultural expression of the church Christ is building."

Eddie has a unique ability to share the gospel message and God's word with deep passion, transparency and humor and a special anointing to lead people in worship. Their daughter, Mandy, and son-in- law, Matt, serve as Youth Pastors of Grace Culture. Their son, Jareb, and his wife, Amanda, are on staff at Elevation Church in Charlotte, North Carolina. If asked, Eddie will say that even though his pride and joy at the present time is his grandson Kaiden, additional grandchildren would be even more wonderful.

Made in the USA
Lexington, KY
09 June 2014